Marketing Is Dead, Long Live Marketing:
Discover the emerging marketing landscape, build effective strategies, and
set your business up for success

Published by Nuanced Media
Tucson, Arizona
Nuancedmedia.com

ISBN: 978-0-578-46525-8
LCCN: 2019934647

CONTENTS

PREFACE
WHY I WROTE THIS BOOK

After losing $300,000 founding and ultimately destroying my first company by doing everything wrong, I have dedicated my life to doing business better, smarter, and faster. During my time at Nuanced Media, we have applied a few lean strategies that focus on the 20 percent that creates 80 percent of the ROI. This includes challenging the existing thought process regarding marketing and business development, implementing the scientific method so we are constantly improving in a trackable manner, and focusing on what really matters—the profitability of our partners' businesses. In the new digital business-development world, systems and infrastructure are being established that can be tested and optimized, which ultimately lead to a sustainable strategic advantage for industry leaders. As we have recently seen with the manufacturing industry's automation to reduce cost and increase efficiency and revenue, the same is occurring with businesses throughout the world.

This book is intended to be an introduction to some of the new methods and philosophies of digital business development/profit engineering. We are in the middle of a very large paradigm shift, and one needs to start at the beginning.

GLOSSARY
KEY ACRONYMS AND TERMS

PPC: PPC stands for pay-per-click and is used to promote products and services. In short, you pay a network to display adverts on their network. Whenever a visitor clicks on the advert, you are charged money by the network.

SEO: SEO stands for Search Engine Optimization. Search engine optimization is the practice of increasing the quantity and quality of traffic to your website through organic search engine results, such as on Google.

Google Adwords: Google Ads is Google's online advertising program. Through Google Ads, you can create online ads to reach people exactly when they're interested in the products and services that you offer.

Inbound Marketing: Inbound marketing is a technique for drawing customers to products and services via content marketing, social media marketing, search engine optimization, and branding.

Outbound Marketing: Outbound marketing refers to any kind of marketing where a company initiates the conversation and sends a message out to its audience. Examples of outbound marketing include TV commercials, radio ads, and print advertisements.

Facebook Ads: Facebook ads are targeted to users based on their location, demographics, and profile information on Facebook. Many of these options are only available on Facebook. After creating an ad, you set a budget and bid for each click or thousand impressions that your ad will receive. Users then see your ads in the sidebar on Facebook.com.

ROI: Return on investment is a ratio between the net profit and cost of investment resulting from an investment of some resources. A high ROI means the investment's gains favorably to its cost.

B2B Marketing: Business-to-business marketing involves the sale of one company's product or service to another company. In short, it means you are selling your product or service to another business, not directly to a consumer.

B2C Marketing: Business-to-consumer marketing focuses on selling to individuals (consumers) and marketing products for personal use.

Content Marketing: Content marketing is a strategic marketing approach focused on creating and distributing valuable and relevant content to attract and retain an audience. This can be done through videos, blogs, emails and more.

Social Media Marketing: Social media marketing (SMM) refers to techniques that target social networks and applications to spread brand awareness and promote particular products. Some popular social media marketing channels include Facebook, Twitter, LinkedIn, Instagram and Pinterest.

Lead Generation: Lead generation is the initiation of consumer interest or inquiry into products or services of a business. Leads can be created for numerous different purposes such as list building or for sales leads. There are many different digital lead generation platforms.

SECTION 1 | ATTRACTION

ATTRACTION

BUSINESS SCHOOL DEFINITION

Making potential clients aware of your product or service

PROFIT ENGINEERING DEFINITION

In the traditional sense of the word, attraction = marketing. Attract people to your brand, whatever that brand offers or represents

Measurement and tracking are key during this phase. If you don't know how somebody found you, you can never optimize your business development structure because you won't know where to best focus your efforts.

PART 1
MARKETING IS DEAD
EXECUTIVE SUMMARY

In this section, we'll discuss:

- How much marketing has changed in the past quarter century; we need to use a different word for the tasks involved.

- The specifics of what changed in B2B marketing and why.

- Changes in the modern consumer that make old-school marketing ineffective, and even alienating.

CHAPTER 1

THE M-WORD

The process started with Carole showing our team everything they had going on with their marketing, and there was a lot of it. They had a company blog, which was shared out across LinkedIn and Google Plus. They used SEO tools to bring in Google traffic and a host of PPC and PPI ads to give those efforts a boost. They advertised in several industry magazines, bought a booth at the three biggest trade shows for the year, and had direct snail mail and email programs for a mailing list of tens of thousands.

It had all worked like a well-oiled machine until two years ago, and we all knew why. Then it stopped working. I knew why that happened too.

"The problem is that all of your marketing is outdated, and you aren't tracking what's working and what isn't," I told her when we sat down to teleconference.

"We create new messaging every month," Carole countered.

"But you haven't updated how you market," I said. "Old-school marketing doesn't take into account the quality of leads or end sales. What's effective has changed drastically, even in this decade. In fact, it's changed so much that I don't even like calling it marketing anymore because it's only part of a much larger system."

"Well, what do you call it?"

"Attraction. Let me tell you why ... "

Don Draper Had It Easy

By the 1960s, marketing and sales had things pretty much dialed in. Even without the big data metrics of today, they knew what worked. They knew why it worked, when to do it, and how much it would cost. For the next thirty years or so, there was little change in the nature of B2B marketing. Business development experts could base their recommendations on years of consistent, unchanging experience.

Then came the internet.

It broke everything. *Everything*. Consumers today aren't just more sophisticated than consumers of the last century. Their buying decision processes have changed completely. Vendors can't rely on "Act Fast! Crazy Prices!" sales-speak anymore or even the keyword-stuffing practices of yester-decade. Everything substantive has changed, especially in the B2B world.

A 2011 study of six hundred CEOs and decision-makers by London-based Fournaise Marketing Group found that 70 percent of CEOs thought their CMOs lacked business credibility. Those CEOs were tired of being told to spend money on returns they were told couldn't be directly measured *and* that traditional marketing techniques were consistently less effective with each passing year.

We'll spend a lot of time going into the details of what changed, why you should care, and what you can do about it. For now, we'll focus on the most important shift in your responsibilities as a successful business leader.

Interruption Killed It

As we'll see in the next chapter, the overwhelming majority of marketing in the mass-media age has been interruptive. Examples of interruptive marketing include:

- ✓ Direct mail
- ✓ Billboards
- ✓ TV spots
- ✓ Radio ads
- ✓ Telemarketing
- ✓ Spam emails

These are called interruptive marketing because they *interrupt* recipients. Direct mail hits when recipients go to their mailboxes. TV spots cut into the action of shows. Telemarketers call during dinner. Interruptive marketing gets quick results when it does hit but has low ROI because it doesn't target a specific audience well. It's like throwing a lot of darts at a board while blindfolded. You're likely to hit *something* but may or may not hit the bull's-eye.

And there's a good chance you'll annoy a bunch of people while you do it.

The vast amount of information on the internet has changed how companies interact with potential clients and how potential clients interact with vendors. These changes have given birth to the rise of value-added marketing, a key part of the profit engineering process. It has fundamentally changed buying decisions.

That middle step of the process is now self-directed for most B2B decision-makers. Instead of being spurred to action by interruptive claims,[1] prospective buyers go online to review products, read reports, research solutions, and track pricing trends. Where last-century consumers were told what to buy, modern buyers *educate themselves*.

This fundamental change in how people make buying decisions is at the heart of successful marketing in this century. It's also at the heart of the most common mistakes businesses make in approaching prospective clients:

✓ They treat social media as a broadcast platform, essentially turning an interactive tool into an interruptive soapbox.

✓ They focus on SEO tricks and other forms of digital snake oil at the expense of providing valuable, helpful content.

✓ They talk only about themselves instead of the needs and interests of their core demographic.

✓ They only offer the choices to buy something or go away, missing the opportunity to start a meaningful dialogue.

---

1   Of varying degrees of veracity.

It's not all bad news. You'll see throughout this book how this changed modality produces leads who have qualified themselves by telling you exactly what they want and why and who will give you a chance to demonstrate why yours is the best company to provide it. You'll learn how a strong website that educates will turn strangers into leads, leads into buyers, and buyers into brand advocates—all while your staff is asleep at home or busy filling other orders.

If interruptive marketing is throwing darts while blindfolded, strong value-added content is taking careful aim with a single throw. It takes longer and requires more skill, but you know you have the right target, and you have a much better chance of hitting your mark.

Networking Was an Accomplice

When talking with B2B clients about their lead and contact generation, I get the same answer from almost everyone.

> " *We do a lot of trade shows, and we try to encourage referrals."*

Trade shows and referrals have been the bread and butter of B2B marketing *efforts* for more than a century, but you can't say the same for *results*. When I ask those same clients how many new sales they've gotten from all those trade shows and their sweet referral offer, faces get frowny. At best, I get a stammered response about how those things are "hard to measure," or the results are "indirect."

In fact, they're easy to measure. I will spend a lot of time in the pages that follow diving into exactly what to measure, why it matters, and what those measurements can tell you.

The sad truth about face-to-face contact marketing has been the same for as long as it's been around because the time spans for those trade shows are too short to develop real relationships. The internet provides opportunities to extend that contact into something that can bear fruit. It creates new opportunities, and if you leverage it right, the internet lets you make much more out of those referral and trade show leads you do find.

A (Partial) Solution

This book is about how you can direct your media teams to turn these shifts in the marketing landscape from a liability to an asset.

I won't waste your time with detailed tutorials for each step. You have people for that.[2] Instead, I plan to provide you with enough information to give effective orders and to tell when a staffer or consultant has hornswoggled you. Your job isn't to know how the engine works. It's to drive the car as effectively as possible.

---

2   And if you don't, there's always YouTube.

CHAPTER 2
A BRIEF HISTORY OF B2B MARKETING

"But I already understand how marketing works," Chuck said. "I have an MBA and years of experience to prove that. I must tell you, Ryan, that the last twenty years have put me in a room with too many people with new ideas that don't work. What is this attraction you're talking about, other than just slapping a new label on something I already understand?"

"Why should we trust what you're telling us?" Carole added. "Everybody and their pet rabbit are saying they have the solution."

"Because you understand how marketing works," I told them. "Old-school marketing worked because of a combination of features surrounding how people consumed media."

"The good old days of mass-market communication," Chuck said.

"Well, the really old days. In this decade, the 'old days' are anything between 1995 and 2009," I said.

"What happened in 1995?" asked Carole.

"The internet happened, and it changed everything."

Marketing through the Decades

Chances are, as a CEO, you're already familiar with some of the history of business and marketing. There's an equal chance that your education didn't look at that history through the lens of what happened next.

Some of the wunderkinder in your marketing and digital departments know this material backward and forward. They grew up in the middle of it. For those of us who went to B-school *before* this all happened, here's the just-the-facts version.[3]

The Early Days of Marketing

Once upon a time, people generated customers by being near them. The blacksmith sold horseshoes to the people in town, and the local pub sold beer to the people in the neighborhood. Marketing was personal and direct because communication technology provided no other option. Town criers were the closest thing we had to interruptive marketing.

Then came mass-market communication, starting in 1450 when Gutenberg invented movable type. This was first applied to the Bible but soon saw use for broadsheets and flyers. Magazines and newspapers followed fast behind. Print advertising wasn't used only to sell products but also to sell *ideas*. The American and French Revolutions both gained much of their momentum from printed tracts passed quietly from hand to hand. By 1900, print-media marketing was firmly established.

Starting in the 1920s, radio hit the scene. It was joined by television in 1942, when Bulova Watch Company sponsored the first TV commercial. It took just three years after that first commercial for TV to surpass print as the premier advertising medium. Telemarketing soon followed.

Though these new technologies fundamentally changed how advertising *looked*, they didn't really touch how advertising *worked*. Just like the print posters stuck on London walls, they were interruptive declarations of a brand's quality, availability, and price. They talked *at* consumers, not *to* them.

---

3   And for those of us who remember hearing "Just the facts, ma'am" spoken on TV.

The digital age came into its own in 1984[4] with Apple's release of the Macintosh. The internet was still a decade off and social media even further away, but computers immediately began to change how advertising worked. Desktop publishing led to an explosion in print advertising, even as cable and broadcast TV displaced newspapers as the largest ad medium in the United States.

But it was the internet that really did it. The World Wide Web broke big in the mid-'90s, leading to a rapid succession of innovations and discoveries:

✓ April 1994: Canter and Siegel, a Phoenix law firm, posts a message to several thousand newsgroups at once, inventing spam.

✓ 1995: Yahoo and AltaVista become the first search engines.

✓ 1997: The number of people searching for products on the web reaches seventy million.

✓ 1999: Brad Fitzpatrick launches LiveJournal, pushing blogging to the edges of mainstream culture.

By 2000, the "dot-com bubble" had burst, but the internet already had gained all the traction it needed. Over 413 million people were regularly online, and every major corporation had some kind of website. The web was with us to stay.

And things were about to get even more interesting.

New Money for Old Ideas

Pay-per-click advertising broke big in 2000 when Google introduced AdWords, a service to facilitate ads appearing on websites to entice users to click over to advertiser's sites. In 2003, spam had become so pervasive that Congress passed a law restricting unsolicited email advertising. The next year, establishment of the National Do Not Call Registry demonstrated how ubiquitous telemarketing had become.

---

4   The same year *Neuromancer* was released, the seminal cyberpunk novel that featured "cyberspace," a worldwide online space. Make of that what you will.

Although those events showed a changing landscape, they pointed to two inescapable conclusions:

1. Most marketers weren't using new methods. They were simply applying old methods to new media.
2. People were getting fed up with those old methods.

Fortunately,[5] analytics was beginning to suggest a better way to apply the new technologies.

The Age of Digital Marketing

The years between 2004 and 2011 saw refinements in how search engines presented websites and how web searchers interacted with search engines. Although Google[6] did little to share the behind-the-scenes algorithms that drove both ends of these refinements, smart and observant marketers connected many of the most important dots.

✓ Sites containing words or phrases used in searches ranked higher for those searches.

✓ Pages with links leading to them from other pages ranked higher.

✓ Grammar, value, good writing, and even accuracy were secondary concerns.

This led to business models like content mills and legal-advice pages that basically applied the concept of spam to the Google age. Sites blanketed the web with pages flooded with specific search terms that offered questionable value to people looking for that information. Snake-oil types used gray-hat and black-hat techniques, like blocks of search terms in a color that matched a page's background, or paying for thousands of meaningless comments throughout the web with links pointing to their pages.

This was the beginning of SEO, which I'm sure you've heard of.

5   For some.
6   By 2004, Google represented 56.4 percent of web-search traffic, rising to just over 90 percent in 2011.

Small businesses got thousands of new leads using these techniques. New business models made millions. The customers got lots of information—but not much value—from an internet full of pages observing the *letter* of the Google search law while ignoring its *spirit*.

Then, in 2011, Google flexed its muscles.

The Pandapocalypse

Gaming a system is fine and dandy until somebody changes the rules of the game. In early 2011, Google did exactly that by introducing an algorithm update, code named Panda. The update rendered questionable content unhelpful and actively punished most of the common gray-hat and black-hat techniques.

This was terrible news for most SEO "experts"[7] and for businesses that used their techniques. As the new, improved internet adjusted, it was great news for consumers. The post-Panda internet rewarded good-faith efforts to provide high-quality, topical content for people who needed it.

I'm going to say that again, because it will be a key part of understanding everything in this book:

> ❝ *Provide high-quality, relevant content for people who need it.*

Businesses needed to do that because nobody was going to listen to interruptive marketing anymore. Just look at the record:

- ✓ By 2011, watching TV via DVR devices like TEVO reached 42% of the market, owing mostly to being able to skip through commercials.

- ✓ That same year, San Francisco banned the unsolicited distribution of the Yellow Pages.

- ✓ Also in 2011, internet usage surpassed screen time spent watching TV for generations X, Y, and Z.

---

7   Though the smartest and most observant had seen it coming and already adjusted their strategies accordingly.

Put another way, the instant people found out they could skip interruptive advertising and focus on content they valued, they did exactly that. *They ignored ads and went for the good stuff.*

This put modern business growth in an environment where two factors rule every decision:

1. Consumers demand high-quality, relevant content from anybody who wants to hold their attention.

2. Google, the company connecting consumers with content, also demands high-quality, relevant content.

You didn't get where you are today by *not* reading the writing on the wall, so I'm not going to repeat that core message a third time. Instead, I'll spend the rest of this book showing you how to provide, track, and leverage that content.

Future Shock and Changing Times

In 1970, Alvin Toffler wrote *Future Shock*, a book about how rapidly things would change in coming decades. His core concept was that the rate of change was, and would continue to be, accelerating. If you picked up a marketer from 1750 and dropped them in 1850, they would be able to succeed after only a little adjustment because things hadn't really changed all that much. Drop them in 1950, and mass media would render useless almost everything they knew. It would take two hundred years of time travel to put them out of their element.

But if you picked up a marketer from 1950 and dropped them in 2000, they would be completely confused just fifty years into their future.

And techniques golden in 2007? Not just useless but actively harmful just five years later.

That's why it's important for you, as a C-level executive, to understand the whys and core concepts of marketing in the new age. The technology changes faster than the underlying concepts; as long as you keep abreast of trends and broad changes, you can let your team handle the details.

CHAPTER 3
MODERN CONSUMERS

Chuck said, "It's so frustrating. We had this dialed in ten years ago, six years ago, even five years ago. But now we're hemorrhaging sales, and I don't know what to do about it."

"Well, what's the first thing you tell a new member of your sales team? Or the first thing you ask an experienced interviewee about sales?"

"We talk about customers."

"Right. Because it's important to understand your customers. The degree to which a salesperson understands a potential client is the degree to which the sale is likely," I replied. "And what if I told you that you no longer understand your customers?"

"Yes, we do. Carole gave you key customer profiles when we had our first informational meeting."

"You did, and yours was better than most. But there's an aspect of most customers out there today that your profiles and approach miss."

"And what is that?"

"Digital consumers."

"Sounds like a buzzword."

"A little bit, but it's not. You know about digital nomads?"

"You mean telecommuting workers who travel around the world, and turn in their assignments from places like Bali and Amsterdam?"

"Yes. It's a real thing and benefits both employers and employees. Understanding the digital-consumer trend is a lot the same. Here, let me explain ..."

"Keep your friends close, and your enemies closer" is an old saying, but you should keep your *customers* so close that your friends and enemies seem far away by comparison.

Marketing, no matter in what era, is only as effective as your knowledge of who's going to buy your product. As I said in the last chapter, today's potential clients are a completely different animal from those of the last decade. That new animal is ...

✓ Busy

✓ Empowered

✓ Mobile

✓ Social

✓ Impatient

Each of these traits represents a shift from the twentieth century, when consumers accepted the interruptive marketing model. Those consumers had more free time, less access to information, and fewer social connections. They had just one screen in the living room,[8] and would watch commercials if they didn't want a snack or need to pee.

But what do these changes mean in terms of measurable results to build a strategy around? What can they tell us about how to change our business development focus? How can they predict what consumers will look like twenty, ten, or even two years from today?

Busy Consumers

Recent research into consumer time shows us an interesting paradox. Compared to forty years ago, people in wealthy countries, like the United States, work about ten hours less each week to pay their bills. However, poll after poll finds that people feel like they have *less* time than ever before.

Ask one hundred different experts why this is, and you'll get one

---

8   Often just one in the entire home.

hundred different answers.[9] Some posit that more time spent being social online gives less time for engaging in the "real" world. Others suggest that it has to do with off-hour commitments to hobbies, child-rearing, and other pursuits, leaving everybody working more even though they're not getting paid for that work.

Whatever the underlying reasons, there's a takeaway from this paradox: *Consumers feel like they have less time.* Less time for sleep. Less time to exercise. Less time with their families. Less time for vacation, reading, television …

Less time to waste being interrupted by marketing.

Consumers will spend two hours deeply researching a potential purchase and resent a thirty-second ad spot that pops up for the very product they're researching.

Before you create or approve any kind of material, ask yourself if it provides value or simply blares your message while stealing a potential buyer's dearly held time.

Empowered Consumers

There was a time when a broadcast commercial claiming that nine out of ten doctors recommended a product would convince people to buy that product. It worked because that ad spot was the only easy source of information about the product. That is no longer the case.

With instant access to vast amounts of knowledge, available day and night, every day of the year, today's consumers will see those ads and immediately grab their cell phones. They will message two doctors they've friended on Facebook to see what they think of the product. They'll look at Amazon reviews and check out the company with betterbusinessbureau.com and the Ripoff Report. They'll google the study and find out which ten doctors participated and how much the nine were each paid to give that particular opinion.

A partial list of the resources instantaneously available to modern consumers includes:

---

9   Two hundred, if you come back in a year and ask them again.

✓ Wikipedia

✓ Google searches for reports

✓ Amazon product reviews

✓ Blogs on industry topics

✓ Videos and podcasts

✓ Consumer watch sites

✓ Government record reports

✓ Social media reviews and conversations

✓ Direct interaction with representatives of products

✓ Direct interaction with former employees of companies

Few things demonstrate how powerful this new access to information is than the existence of the term *showrooming*.

Showrooming is going into a store for the sole purpose of checking out an item in person before ordering it online. In 2013, a Gallup poll showed that 40 percent of American consumers said they had showroomed at least once. Conservative estimates put the cost to physical retailers in the tens of millions annually from lost potential sales.

If people are willing to use the tools at their disposal for items they've already decided to buy, they can't be relied on to just accept the assertions of your marketing material about things they might not even want.

This change in the relationship between consumers and information demands a reciprocal change in marketing strategy. Make it easy for digital consumers to confirm that your business is trustworthy and transparent. Build deserved trust and thought leadership to convert modern buyers from skeptical observers to brand evangelists.

Mobile Consumers

Mobile devices represent the most profound change in the nature of marketing since the invention of movable type. They have increased tremendously since the advent of the iPhone in 2007. Between 2009 and 2013, ownership of smartphones grew by 300 percent, and tablet ownership went up by twice that amount. Each month, typical Americans use smartphones for just over thirty-four hours to browse the mobile web or engage with apps.

Forget empowerment about *what kind* of information consumers can access. The advent of mobile devices lets consumers decide exactly *where* and *when* they avail themselves of that access.

For example, the modern living room has in it, on average, a number of screens equal to or greater than the number of people currently in the room. If what's on the TV isn't topical, useful, or engaging, consumers will just look down at their phones and find something that is.

In 2013, the Nielsen media survey stopped asking if consumers used their phones or tablets during commercial breaks. Instead, they started asking what they did on those mobile devices during commercials. The question itself tells us a lot about consumer behavior in this decade, but some of the answers gave us even more information:

- ✓ 41% of tablet owners looked up information on actors, plotlines, and other facets of the shows they were watching.

- ✓ 23% emailed, texted, or messaged friends about the programs.

- ✓ 18% read discussions about the shows on social media.

- ✓ 14% bought products or services being advertised during the shows.

For companies clinging to the old interruptive model of advertising, mobile devices are a death sentence. It means nobody can be forced to interact with their content ever again.

But for those who understand and implement value-added, well-engineered marketing strategies, mobility gives consumers the ability to continue interacting with your content whenever the mood strikes.

Your job is to keep them in the mood.

Potential clients want information about your product not only *when* and *where* they want it but also in the format they like best. Make sure you convey your value-added content in a variety of media and your website is responsive to all types of devices.

MOBILEGEDDON

On april 21, 2015, google launched an update to their search engine algorithms that significantly penalizes websites unresponsive to mobile devices. This means if your site doesn't work well on a phone or tablet, you don't exist for google.

Social Consumers

Nearly half of smartphone owners visit social networks daily, and almost two-thirds of social media users say they use those platforms every day. This goes far beyond just cat photos and food porn. A variety of studies over the past five years have demonstrated the extensive influence and power of the social community on buyer behavior:

- ✓ 71% of consumers report being more likely to make a purchase if referred or recommended via social media.

- ✓ When American Eagle added a Facebook Like button to every product on their site, they saw a 57% increase in average purchase size.

- ✓ Products with fifty or more reviews on popular consumer sites like Amazon.com experience 65% more sales than comparable products with fewer than five reviews.

✓ Facebook is the number 1 influencer on consumer decisions about baby products, Twitter number 1 for electronics and YouTube number 1 for music.

✓ 70% of social network users shop online, which is 12% higher than the general average.

✓ 84% of millennial shoppers say consumer-written content influences what they buy.

✓ Mobile shoppers who view customer content reviews have a 133% higher conversion rate than those who do not.

The power of social media for engaged brands is nearly impossible to overstate, as is how disruptive and destructive ignoring the power of social communication can be. As a top-level manager or business owner, you don't need to know the details of what happens in the social space. You have people for that. But you must understand its importance and how to read key metrics that tell you how well those people are doing their jobs.

Want the opposite of a well–thought-out social media campaign? Run a YouTube search for John Oliver's piece on Starbucks' "Race Together" initiative. It's a perfect example of how *not* to engage on social media.

Impatient Consumers (Aren't Always Impatient)

So far, I've painted a picture of mobile-empowered, multiscreened, web-browsing potential clients who will flit away from your content the instant it stops being of value.

This is accurate, but it's not the whole picture.

These same consumers will spend all the time they need, ask every conceivable question, and research for months when waffling between thinking about buying and actually making purchases. Because of this, they represent both challenges and opportunities for modern business managers.

The challenges we've already discussed. Relying on old interruptive models that add no value will lose you any chance of beginning dialogues with them. You must understand what they need and provide it. They want content they will read on purpose, engage with online, and tell their colleagues about. You can't simply broadcast content—even good content—and expect it to impact them.

The opportunity here comes from the exponential power of having a bank of quality content anybody can access, at their convenience, at any time. Modern consumers are impatient with salespeople, salesspeak, and sales pitches. They will not trust anyone who begins a conversation with an attempt to make a sale. They want real relationships with people they can see as mentors, coaches, experts, or fellow enthusiasts.[10] If you can build this rapport online and automatically, via content that buyers find for themselves, your qualification and conversion rates will skyrocket.

10   Best of all.

PART 2
INBOUND KILLED THE OUTBOUND STAR
EXECUTIVE SUMMARY

In this section, we'll discuss:

- The difference between outbound and inbound marketing

- How inbound marketing has changed what works and what doesn't in consumer attraction

- What this shifting paradigm means to business owners and marketing managers worldwide

---

CHAPTER 4
INBOUND VS. OUTBOUND MARKETING

"Okay, okay," Chuck replied. "That makes sense, but what do we do about it?"

"The whole machine is very complex, with a lot of moving parts."

"Try me. I'm a smart guy. I didn't get where I am by being afraid to learn new things."

"No, you didn't, but you did get there by knowing what to make your problem and what to make somebody else's responsibility. You're setting the route. Your team works on the engine, changes the oil, and drives the car."

"I … I resemble that remark."

"Good. So what you need is the map to your destination. Your team will handle the rest."

"I'm guessing you're going to provide that map."

"Good guess. Sticking with the car metaphor, this is a lot like the changes that happened when they put in the interstate freeway system. Old highways still run here and there. They're interesting but slow-going. A smart road trip sticks to the freeways. The old highways are outbound marketing."

"And the freeways are?"

"Inbound."

I mentioned in the last chapter how outbound marketing[11] is either dead or sliding toward death. Though print, radio, and television spots still generate some return, only people with an interest in keeping the paradigm alive recommend marketing strategies that rely on these twentieth-century methods.

We know this because consumers have spoken loud and clear on two fronts about how fed up they are with interruptive methods. They've voted with both their attention spans and their dollars and given clearly superior responses to inbound marketing methods.

Further, they've voted with their … um, well, with their votes. The fed-upness of modern Americans has pushed legislators into passing a variety of laws limiting or forbidding some of the most common forms of interruptive advertising. A brief timeline of the trends and legislation illustrating this shift includes:

- ✓ 2003: The CAN-SPAM Act forbids unsolicited email advertising.

- ✓ 2004: The National Do Not Call List is created. By the end of the year, 66% of the US population is on the list.

- ✓ 2006: Google's personalized search function suspends new signups because the huge demand is crashing the system.

- ✓ 2011: DVR viewing surpasses TV viewing, with "skipping commercials" cited as a key reason.

- ✓ 2011: San Francisco bans distribution of unsolicited Yellow Pages.

- ✓ 2011: For younger demographics, internet screen time exceeds time spent watching television.

True, there is a sort of habituation going on with interruptive advertising. With the exception of telemarketing, few consumers report that this well-established type of marketing actually alienates them. We've grown accustomed to it, and some models are still going strong.

---

11   a.k.a. *interruptive* marketing.

The best example of this in action is the preroll ads on YouTube.[12] These are both interruptive and outbound but can increase conversion rates by up to 20 percent because they are targeted specifically to people likely to watch the video that follows.

As you'll see later, it's possible to design your inbound marketing system to make lower-cost leads significantly more qualified than leads gathered via interruptive, outbound methods. More on that in a bit. Right now, let's look at what we mean by outbound and inbound marketing. What are they? How are they different? How are they similar? What makes consumers so responsive to one and blasé about the other?

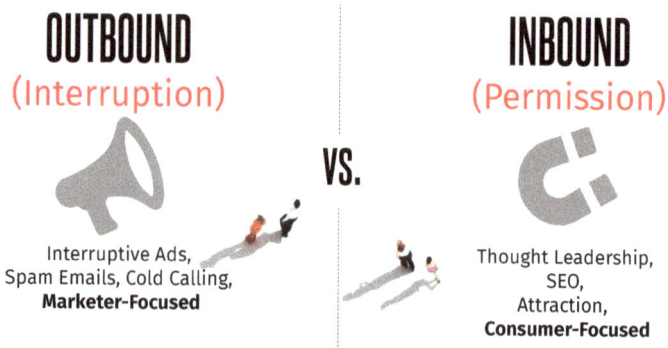

OUTBOUND
(Interruption)

VS.

INBOUND
(Permission)

Interruptive Ads,
Spam Emails, Cold Calling,
Marketer-Focused

Thought Leadership,
SEO,
Attraction,
Consumer-Focused

Outbound vs. Inbound 101

In broad strokes, *outbound* marketing was about telling consumers what they wanted and directing them to a place where they could buy that thing. It was kind of Orwellian, when you think about it.

Inbound marketing is about listening to buyers telling you what they want and then providing answers to their questions about that thing. It's more like consultation or education than sales. Potential clients have some kind of pain, and they are searching the internet for a cure. They find your content (be it a web page, e-book, webinar, social media post, or whatever). The content helps them ease their pain, and they look to you as an expert on how to solve it entirely.

---

12   Those video spots you wait five seconds on before continuing to your cat video.

Drilling down a bit, we can see this play out in a variety of traits of modern consumers.

New Digital Consumers ...

Do Their Own Research

Outbound marketing worked in the last century because average consumers had limited access to information. If an ad spot made a claim, consumers had to accept it as truth. An ad making a false claim in this decade gets caught within moments of broadcasting the message. That by itself represents an important change in the landscape.

More important, strong profit engineers understand their best bet is in *helping consumers do that research*. This sets your brand up in the position of coach, adviser, mentor, and expert. It also lets you benefit from the outbound efforts of the competition because buyers will use your material to research the claims made by others.

Are Aggressively Mobile

Outbound marketing took powerful advantage of captive audiences during its heyday. With the advent of smartphones, those captive audiences simply don't exist.

Inbound marketing lets consumers hold their own attention by offering content they decided to search for. This means you don't have to fight the modern mobile mind by trying to force somebody to pay attention. Instead, you *work with* consumers by hacking that tendency to check in ... by becoming the place potential customers check into.

Are Socially Active

Word of mouth has been a powerful force since well before outbound marketing was even a thing. During the days when outbound was king, advertising capitalized on this both by encouraging referrals and through implied word of mouth in the form of testimonials from celebrities and paid experts.[13] Social media has fundamentally changed how word of mouth works.

---

13   "Nine out of ten doctors recommend ..."

A single disgruntled client on social media could poison your well for thousands. A delighted brand advocate could bring in hundreds of sales a year. More than any other aspect of modern digital buyers, this ability to push or destroy sales has changed how business growth works.

You Must Remember This

Put simply, outbound general marketing was the best choice during the twentieth-century age of *broadcast media*. It got your message out to vast numbers and trusted that wide coverage to net a handful of interested consumers.

Inbound marketing is the best choice for twenty-first-century business development. It leverages the changes in modern media and consumers to connect you with the most interested and qualified people ready to make buying decisions.

It's also important to remember that inbound campaigns *add value* in ways that broadcast campaigns simply can't. They give potential buyers access to information, education, and advice beyond the scope of even the broadest broadcast media. This factor is vital to the success of your efforts, since it's the foundation of the mentor-student relationship you want to develop with anybody interested in your product.

CHAPTER 5
WHAT IS INBOUND MARKETING?

"You know what you're starting to sound like?" Chuck said.

"What?"

"A damned consultant. You've revved me up with all this talk about change, and now you're going to tell me about some miracle solution that's so complex only you can implement it. You'll charge me an arm and a leg and then ask for my CFO's arm too."

"Nope."

"What do you mean 'nope'?"

"The solution's pretty simple. It's called profit engineering. By the time we're done, you'll probably be able to do it on your own for free."

"Profit engineering?"

"Profit engineering is a complete business development solution that looks at your whole business funnel and targets the 20 percent that will make you 80 percent of the return. There are a few moving parts to profit engineering. Let's start with why inbound marketing is such a powerful and important part of profit engineering and go from there."

By now you understand why changes in the landscape of business development and the makeup of this century's consumers make inbound marketing the best method for gaining and keeping new customers.

Understanding *why* this is so is your next step in learning how to engineer the growth of your company effectively. To do that, we need to look deeply at what inbound marketing actually is.

The 2010s Marketing Crisis

There is a serious crisis in marketing in this decade. Old methods no longer work, not even when companies double their spending on previously reliable methods.

This crisis isn't just a bit of marketing buzzword trickery to bandy about at conventions. It's deadly serious, impacting and even closing business every year because of four damaging factors:

- ✓ Customers are tired of interruptive, non-value–adding advertising media.

- ✓ Customers have become inured to sales-speak like "limited-time offer" and authority-based marketing.

- ✓ Customers control how often and how deeply they consume media, including advertising spots.

- ✓ Customers are deeply suspicious of any communication that tries to rush them into or otherwise pressure sales.

To make matters worse, many marketing "experts" recommend applying old concepts to new technologies. They treat fundamentally interactive social and web platforms as just another soapbox for broadcast interruptive messaging.

This approach neither works nor deserves to work. Companies using these old-school methods out themselves as having no regard for what consumers want and little knowledge about the relationship between modern buyers and the vendors and the products they deal with.

Inbound Marketing: A Solution

By contrast, inbound marketing solves the problems of old-school marketing in myriad ways. It adds value with useful, on-topic content. It invites instead of interrupts, waiting for consumers who are already interested in the products. It adopts an advisory role and tone to avoid the pitfalls of seeming like a salesperson. It invests heavily in consumer control and considers the traits of modern, mobile buyers.

In short, it builds on a foundation of what consumers want, instead of trying to force consumers to want what's offered. This leads to more highly qualified leads in your sales queue and to customers who've been primed from the beginning to become delighted and enthusiastic brand advocates.

A pair of case studies demonstrate the impressive power of inbound marketing.

SoldOut started life in 2009, offering telemarketing services to start-ups throughout Japan as a way to bolster client growth. Over the first four years of its life, it saw lower returns from those telemarketing services, despite rising costs of executing even simple telemarketing initiatives. In 2013, the company pulled the plug on what was obviously a dying modality. Two years later, the company generated as much as fifty times the number of qualified leads monthly for each of its customers. These inbound marketing services, which the company calls "pull" marketing, refer to the inbound tendency to pull customers in rather than push a message out.

Ireland-based Boxever is an SaaS start-up targeting clients in the travel industry. After trying a variety of outbound methods that generated reasonable sales at a reasonable cost, the company applied a landing page app, an email mailing list, and a blog aimed at educating travel industry decision-makers who might be interested in their service. The first year saw a 500 percent increase in leads without increasing ad-spend.

By now, you can see why inbound marketing has taken the lead in many marketing communities. It's the most powerful way to expand a brand's reach and reputation in the marketplace of ideas that is the internet.

But there's a right way and a wrong way to do inbound marketing. Those who just go through the motions will do better than if they never take on inbound as a marketing method, but they won't be able to compete with those who truly understand, embrace, and execute inbound marketing as part of their profit engineering plan.

CHAPTER 6
THE SHIFTING PARADIGM

"So, I want to change my marketing-spend to match new media and new consumers," Chuck said.

"It's bigger than that. You're going to change your marketing-spend to match new media and new consumers, just like you said, but you need to make a more fundamental shift in your thinking."

"You already said that. I'm changing from marketing to business development."

"But you're still thinking of it in terms of marketing. This paradigm shift needs you to view your relationship with customers more like dating. What do you call someone who makes all kinds of romantic gestures just to get someone into bed but then forgets their name and never calls afterward?"

"A jerk."

"Right. How often do your salespeople treat customers the same way?"

"Uh …"

"Exactly. Because of some of the things we've already talked about, you have to be the person who's sincerely into a relationship. The kind of person who sends flowers the morning after and again the next week. There are lots of reasons for that …"

It's time to turn our attention from buyers to the systems that drive your business growth. To do that, we need to talk about the major paradigm shift in marketing in the digital age.

It used to be that marketing was the biggest part of promoting a business or brand. You let people know what you offered and how to reach you. People who wanted what you had came in the door, relied on your advice, and left the building with the product in hand or services rendered. Broadcast interruptive marketing worked well for that. Well enough to be the given the lion's share of the budget.

But things have changed.

Today, marketing is just one part of a complex system of buyer attraction. It's not even the most important part. This shift in paradigm represents an immense change in how acquiring and keeping clients works.

A few of the factors that contributed to this shift include:

✓ The death of correlation marketing. Before, you spent money on marketing and your phone rang. Hooray! Marketing worked … or not. There's a reason *post hoc ergo proctor hoc*[14] is listed among the classical logical fallacies. Your phone might have rung because of the ads, or because of something in the local news, or because of a seasonal surge.

✓ The rise of easy data access. Social media, automated sales reports, and robust analytical reports mean that even small, independent shops can get real, (reasonably) accurate, meaningful data to drive each phase of business development. That the death of correlation marketing occurred at the same time as the advent of easy access to data is not coincidental.

✓ Changes in the sales process. Modern digital buyers have made 57% of their decisions before contacting vendors. They get that far by leveraging easy data access to diagnose, explore, and review options.

---

14 A logical fallacy that states that because event B *followed* event A, it was *caused* by event A.

✓ Transparency. Modern consumers have access to every review anyone has written about you, your product, and your services at the tips of their fingers. We live in a "big town, small universe" world now. If you engage in shady business practices, your potential customers will find out about it.

All of this adds up to needing a new kind of approach to attracting clients. The degree to which you can shift your sales paradigm to match the new customer model is the degree to which your efforts will succeed in this decade and the next.[15]

Changed Thinking on Attraction

The first thing necessary to address this paradigm shift is to stop thinking of what you're doing as "sales" or "marketing." Start thinking about it as part of profit engineering to reflect the comprehensive, top-to-bottom perception you need to deploy with each prospective client.

Second, you must start thinking of customer relationships in the same way you would any other relationships. You would never walk up to a new coworker and say, "Hi. Wanna become best friends and loan me your power tools?" You wouldn't step into a singles bar and shout, "Hey! Who wants to come home with me?" Instead, you invest time and energy in creating relationships where you might end up with new best friends or romantic partners … and if it not, you and the other people will still have gotten some kind of value out of the time you spent together.

Third, starting with the first contact, set up ways to delight customers and motivate them to tell others about the experience. Social, connected mobile consumers are always just ten seconds away from talking about you. Make it easy for them to say nice things.

Fourth, surrender the illusion that you can control any part of the buyer's journey. Those days are long gone. What's worse, customers who see you trying to assert control are likely to find competitors who don't.

---

15   I won't promise success further out than that. Some new game-changer will show up and upset the whole ecosystem. I can promise to see it coming and be among the first to adopt and understand how that impacts all phases of profit engineering.

Instead, you should look for ways to give value at every level, point, or area with which customers decide to spend time interacting.

Fifth, make your primary value to early customers the amount and quality of information you can provide. This is more than implementing a few key action items mentioned earlier. It requires total reassessment of the purposes and delivery of your content and how well your existing content serves those purposes.

Remember a few paragraphs back when I said this was like a relationship? All successful relationships are based on mutual respect. You must have and show respect for buyers by not running "sales games" or gimmicky interruptive marketing. You want to gain and keep respect from buyers by presenting yourself as knowledgeable, truthful, relevant, and fair. Inbound marketing is a process that breeds both.

PART 3
THE NEW BUYER'S JOURNEY
EXECUTIVE SUMMARY

In this section, we'll discuss:

- The basics of the buyer's journey
- How awareness has changed since 2005
- How consideration has changed since 2005
- How decisions have changed since 2000

CHAPTER 7

THE NEW BUYER'S JOURNEY

"Whoa, that is a lot to take in," Chuck said. "I feel like I just tried to drink from a fire hose."

"It's one of those things that's tough to acclimatize to at first, but with a closer look, you'll find a lot of stuff you already know and other stuff you don't know but know enough things like it, so you'll pick it up quickly."

"So you say. It's starting to sound like a consultant spiel again."

"When learning something new, it's often easiest to apply something you already know."

"Yeah, okay."

"You're aware of the buyer's journey."

"You mean awareness, consideration, and decision?"

"Yes."

"Of course. That's first-year B-school stuff right there."

"Okay. Let's map inbound marketing to the three stages of the buyer's journey, and get you an overview of how this might work in a context you already understand."

Stop me if you've heard this one.

Actually, don't.

You've definitely heard this one. It's first-year B-school material, but it's good to think about again in the context of what you've read so far. The buyer's journey has remained the same since people began buying things. But as with all aspects of selling in the twenty-first century, the details have changed significantly.

You know the basics of the old way. Sales reps came to buyers with a general understanding of what buyers in their position needed. They started a conversation, and sometimes that conversation ended with a sale.

Today, buyers diagnose their own problems and research options in advance. A recent CEB study of over 1,400 B2B customers in multiple industries found that 57 percent of purchase decisions get made *before first contact with a vendor.*

Let's look more closely at the three stages of the buyer's journey and what the modern, connected mobile world has done to change them.

Easy as One, Two, Three

Buyers like to think of their situations as unique, but nearly all buying processes go through the same three steps:

THE BUYER'S JOURNEY

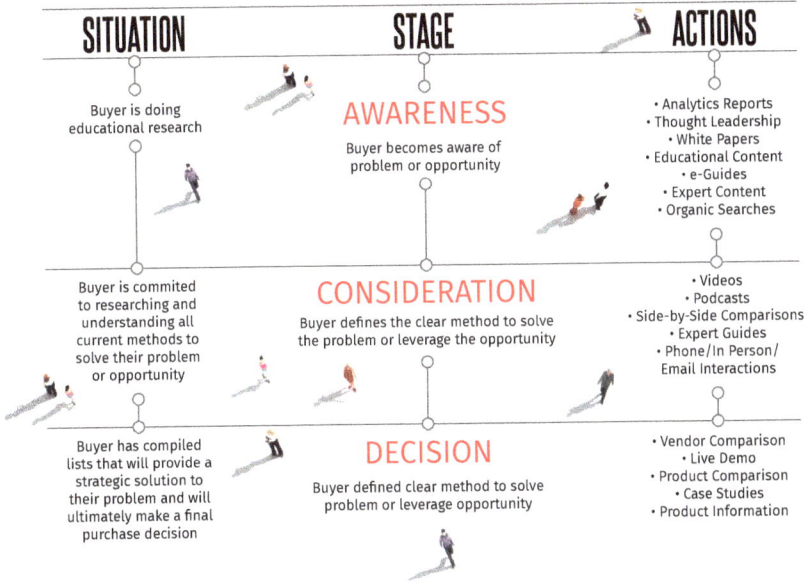

SITUATION	STAGE	ACTIONS
Buyer is doing educational research	**AWARENESS** Buyer becomes aware of problem or opportunity	• Analytics Reports • Thought Leadership • White Papers • Educational Content • e-Guides • Expert Content • Organic Searches
Buyer is commited to researching and understanding all current methods to solve their problem or opportunity	**CONSIDERATION** Buyer defines the clear method to solve the problem or leverage the opportunity	• Videos • Podcasts • Side-by-Side Comparisons • Expert Guides • Phone/In Person/ Email Interactions
Buyer has compiled lists that will provide a strategic solution to their problem and will ultimately make a final purchase decision	**DECISION** Buyer defined clear method to solve problem or leverage opportunity	• Vendor Comparison • Live Demo • Product Comparison • Case Studies • Product Information

This was true in the old days and remains true now. The question is, how do you change your approach to this truism while also meeting how the details have changed?

> **❝** *Awareness—when buyers become aware of a problem or opportunity*

Twenty-first–century buyers are informed and sophisticated, and B2B buyers are expected to know not only what's happening in their areas of responsibility but *what's likely to happen* in the coming months and years. These customers go looking for their own problems and opportunities. Smart profit engineering decisions are those where customers get *involved* with sources of information, setting up vendors to begin the journey as advisers and guides.

> *Consideration—when buyers clearly define the problem or opportunity*

Old-school sales presentations cost—and made—a lot of money, but today's consumers are suspicious of packaged sales pitches and look closely at any claims vendors might make. They prefer to find their own answers by reading expert articles, social reviews, and other online sources of information. Modern strategy creates content that serves as that information source, maintaining that position of guide and adviser, and continues relationships started during the awareness stage.

> *Decision—when buyers have clearly defined the preferred method to solve the problem or leverage the opportunity*

Once upon a time, this was the "Big Finish." Reps asked a closing question and then saw what happened next. If they had provided useful, topical content to buyers during the awareness and consideration stages, they didn't have to ask. Customers had confidence in their expertise, which they'd earned though demonstrating it in their content. Customers would simply accept the advice and take the next logical step: the sale.

The Other Side of the Mountain

Here's a part you probably haven't heard before.

The buyer's journey doesn't stop at decision anymore. In the age of mobile social buyers, stopping once the sale is made is a mistake.

It has always cost five times as much to attract a new lead as to sell to an existing client, but the modern age makes that aftercare even more vital.

If the buyer's journey is a trip up a mountain, and the decision is the peak, you can't just go back down the trail to find another climber. Instead, you need to walk down the other side of the mountain with the new client. Motivate him to tell his friends, relatives, clients, colleagues, mentors, and pets about how great the view is from the top. Only when he's doing that is your job as a guide along the buyer's journey truly complete.

THE BUYER'S JOURNEY

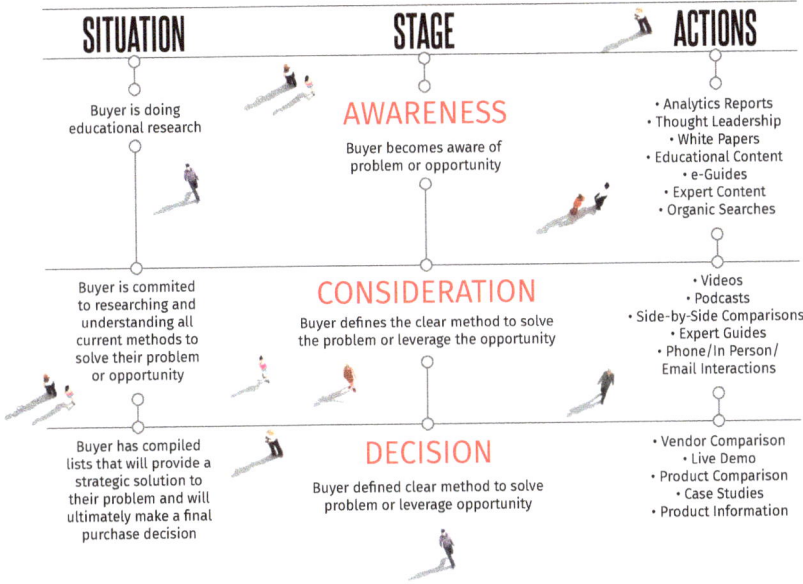

SITUATION	STAGE	ACTIONS
Buyer is doing educational research	**AWARENESS** Buyer becomes aware of problem or opportunity	• Analytics Reports • Thought Leadership • White Papers • Educational Content • e-Guides • Expert Content • Organic Searches
Buyer is commited to researching and understanding all current methods to solve their problem or opportunity	**CONSIDERATION** Buyer defines the clear method to solve the problem or leverage the opportunity	• Videos • Podcasts • Side-by-Side Comparisons • Expert Guides • Phone/In Person/ Email Interactions
Buyer has compiled lists that will provide a strategic solution to their problem and will ultimately make a final purchase decision	**DECISION** Buyer defined clear method to solve problem or leverage opportunity	• Vendor Comparison • Live Demo • Product Comparison • Case Studies • Product Information

This was true in the old days and remains true now. The question is, how do you change your approach to this truism while also meeting how the details have changed?

> *Awareness—when buyers become aware of a problem or opportunity*

Twenty-first–century buyers are informed and sophisticated, and B2B buyers are expected to know not only what's happening in their areas of responsibility but *what's likely to happen* in the coming months and years. These customers go looking for their own problems and opportunities. Smart profit engineering decisions are those where customers get *involved* with sources of information, setting up vendors to begin the journey as advisers and guides.

> *Consideration—when buyers clearly define the problem or opportunity*

Old-school sales presentations cost—and made—a lot of money, but today's consumers are suspicious of packaged sales pitches and look closely at any claims vendors might make. They prefer to find their own answers by reading expert articles, social reviews, and other online sources of information. Modern strategy creates content that serves as that information source, maintaining that position of guide and adviser, and continues relationships started during the awareness stage.

> *Decision—when buyers have clearly defined the preferred method to solve the problem or leverage the opportunity*

Once upon a time, this was the "Big Finish." Reps asked a closing question and then saw what happened next. If they had provided useful, topical content to buyers during the awareness and consideration stages, they didn't have to ask. Customers had confidence in their expertise, which they'd earned though demonstrating it in their content. Customers would simply accept the advice and take the next logical step: the sale.

The Other Side of the Mountain

Here's a part you probably haven't heard before.

The buyer's journey doesn't stop at decision anymore. In the age of mobile social buyers, stopping once the sale is made is a mistake.

It has always cost five times as much to attract a new lead as to sell to an existing client, but the modern age makes that aftercare even more vital.

If the buyer's journey is a trip up a mountain, and the decision is the peak, you can't just go back down the trail to find another climber. Instead, you need to walk down the other side of the mountain with the new client. Motivate him to tell his friends, relatives, clients, colleagues, mentors, and pets about how great the view is from the top. Only when he's doing that is your job as a guide along the buyer's journey truly complete.

✓ Ask clients to invest large blocks of time watching videos, reading e-books, or otherwise interacting with lengthy or mastery-level materials. Buyers are at the primer stage here. They need quick-reading, basic information that informs without intimidating.

✓ Provide material that mentions specific brands, offerings, or solutions. This is step one. That kind of information is helpful later down the road but feels like pressure to buy at this stage.

✓ Use technical terms, jargon, or industry slang—unless it's in the context of a glossary to help introduce readers to important context.

We all have that one friend who's constantly complaining about things but never seems interested in solutions. Although awareness-stage customers usually move forward, you should think of them as exactly like that friend. *Listen* to the symptoms and provide ways for them to diagnose their problems in a low-pressure, information-rich context. Also like that friend, you should avoid alienating them by leaping right into giving unsolicited advice.

At this stage, it's vitally important to remain customer-centric in all decisions about your marketing plan and content. Yes, it's tempting to make this communication about how awesome *you* are. But that message is for later stages. Buyers aren't yet ready to compare you to other vendors. They haven't even decided you're the kind of vendor they need.

PRODUCT GEEKERY

Even those who successfully avoid the "all about me" trap can sometimes fall into being product geeks.

Product geeks are so passionate about what they sell, they assume everybody else is as fascinated with it as they are. They make their content all about the product (or the science behind it) or all about the brand. Again, that's not what awareness-stage buyers are looking for.

All of your content at this stage should be *about the clients*. Tune it toward the questions you anticipate your buyers will ask. Tone it appropriately for their most likely mental state and demographic. Provide answers to the most important questions, stated in terms laypeople can understand.

Awareness-Stage Best Practices

This is an executive-level book, so I won't dive deeply into the details of how to do most of what I'm suggesting. However, it's important for you to understand the most effective best practices so you can make certain your team is applying them.

- ✓ Focus on the common symptoms of the problem your product solves. Be as specific as possible. Never offer a product that isn't perfect for your leads. It erodes trust and implies you aren't listening.

- ✓ Use the kinds of words people use while making initial searches for your product. Don't forget action words like troubleshoot, resolve, upgrade, and optimize.

- ✓ Ask yourself what emotions and events you experienced when you first became interested in what your company offers. What messages, ideas, and content gave you the information you needed? What questions did you not yet know how to ask?

- ✓ Avoid underestimating or condescending to your readers by explaining common knowledge.

- ✓ Avoid providing too much information too quickly. This can overwhelm entry-level leads and alienate them.

- ✓ Provide content that gives strong introductory material without demanding too much from readers. Reports, e-guides and e-books, blog posts, and white papers are excellent examples.

Every part of your content should simultaneously accomplish two goals. It should catch the interest and trust of leads by being a convenient, authoritative source of information, *and* it should establish you, your business, and your website as the go-to source for further information.

In the bad old days, new buyers started shopping after being introduced to a product via interruptive marketing. New digital users start their journey earlier by researching potential causes of some pain, annoyance, or worry. They actively seek thought leadership, actionable advice, and threads to access more information. They want reassurance that they are making the right decision as they take each forward step in the buyer's journey.

The awareness stage is your opportunity to establish a role with buyers, not as a sales representative but rather as a teacher, educator, guide, and coach. Seize this opportunity, and customers will make the decision on their own to buy from you. Miss it, and they will take their business to somebody who listens.

CHAPTER 9
CONSIDERATION AND INFORMED BUYERS

"This next stage is where inbound marketing can really shine," I said.

"How do you mean?" Chuck asked. "This is usually the trickiest part of the journey, where the difference between a good salesman and a great salesman really stands out."

"Tell me more about that."

"The consideration phase is all about negotiating the balance between not making frequent enough contact to stay in the front of the mind for leads and making contact so frequently you become annoying and lose the sale. If you can help with that, this alone might make the paradigm shift you mention worth it."

"That's been our experience too, and yes—inbound marketing shifts the power dynamic in ways that keep customers interested in what you have to say."

"I'm not sure I like that. If you give customers too much power, you might lose the sale simply because they get busy or distracted."

"That's all right, though. Inbound marketing sets up ways to reacquire attention without coming off as overly aggressive. It combines technology and that changed role you set up during awareness to keep the conversation light, noninvasive, and appreciated."

"Okay. I'm still interested. Tell me more."

As buyers get a handle on what might be causing symptoms, they move into the consideration stage. In the overview, we defined consideration as the stage where buyers clearly define the problem or opportunity.

THE BUYER'S JOURNEY

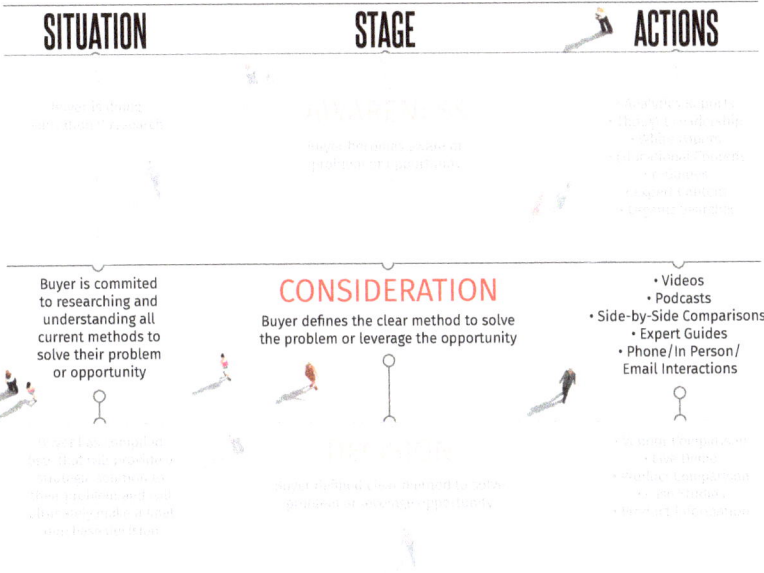

SITUATION	STAGE	ACTIONS
Buyer is commited to researching and understanding all current methods to solve their problem or opportunity	**CONSIDERATION** Buyer defines the clear method to solve the problem or leverage the opportunity	• Videos • Podcasts • Side-by-Side Comparisons • Expert Guides • Phone/In Person/ Email Interactions

At this stage, buyers have analyzed the symptoms they're experiencing. They have a good idea of exactly what is causing those symptoms but are only beginning to research what solutions might exist.

They are not yet seeking detailed, specific information about those solutions, but they will listen to that information if they're still with you, once they become ready.

At this stage, do not use any pressure sales tactics or try to hurry the process. Avoid comparison reports between different solutions, since buyers are not yet ready for that information. At the same time, don't even think about rehashing content buyers have already seen. Keep providing new content.

And keep the content *types* new too. If all you offer is blog posts and white papers, buyers can become bored with your content. Change things up with instructional videos, interactive content, and other "advanced" forms of content. This not only keeps interest up but also gives a sense of graduation or "leveling up" as buyers move farther along.

Consideration-Stage Best Practices

Legendary science fiction author Ray Bradbury once said that ideas are like cats. If you chase them, they'll run away. You have to act like you don't want to pet a cat before it will come over and ask to be petted. This is even more true if you leave a little food nearby.

The same concept applies with buyers at the consideration stage. The more you share information out of a desire to educate or excitement about the industry, the more buyers in this stage will trust what you have to say. By extension, they will trust you and your brand as a source of expertise and quality.

While you're courting buyers, keep in mind some of the established best practices for courting modern buyers:

✓ Focus on the specific issues caused by any given problem, along with a compelling description of what life looks like with that problem solved. This helps buyers realize there's a way out of their current situation and creates a desire for that way out.

✓ Use keywords associated with people who have identified a pain point and are looking for solutions. Some of these will be generally applicable, like service, supplier, tool, and answer. Others will be specific to your industry.

✓ Ask yourself what information you wish you had known when you were at the consideration stage for your last major purchase. Think about what specific questions have turned up in your comments, social media, and sales floor. All of these can inspire new topics for content.

✓ Avoid going too deep, too soon. By this point, it's likely *you* are excited about both the pending sale and how cool your product

is. But *the clients* are still researching, learning, and figuring out what questions to ask. They aren't ready for answers and will view volunteered answers as a high-pressure tactic.

✓ Provide content that gives deeper information on a narrower topic. Webcasts, podcasts, videos, white papers, and live coaching sessions are helpful at this stage. You can also provide several paths or verticals of content, one each for the various problems your product or service solves.

As digital buyers continue their journey toward a final decision and purchase, they need change. Too often, digital marketers aim their content only at awareness-stage buyers.

This is a serious mistake, since it essentially abandons buyers just as they move closer to making an actual purchase.

The consideration stage is your opportunity to cement your relationship as a thought leader and subject-matter expert. As customers move out of this phase and toward a buying decision, the degree to which they perceive you as knowledgeable and helpful is the degree to which they will prefer to make that purchase from you.

CHAPTER 10
THE DECISION

Chuck said, *"That brings us to the sale itself. Are you going to tell me profit engineering replaces a good sales team?"*

"No. Not at all. But it will change how they do their job. Profit engineering includes offering things like buyer's guides, A/B examples, and a call to action that generates sales on its own. But for the serious selling, you'll still be relying on professional human beings."

"I'd say that reduces the value a bit. You wouldn't buy a car that always stops a mile from your house."

"That would depend on how pretty the walk was … but offering inbound content as part of a profit engineering strategy makes the job of your sales team much easier in a variety of ways."

"That's a song I've heard before. How is this different?"

"We'll talk about some of that in detail later, but for now, let's talk about how every single piece of information you provide at this stage helps customers make decisions. It establishes trust and reinforces the relationship. Here's how …"

The final stage of the buyer's journey comes when buyers have clearly defined their preferred method of solving a problem or leveraging an opportunity. They have made a decision to buy[17] and are now choosing which option to purchase.

THE BUYER'S JOURNEY

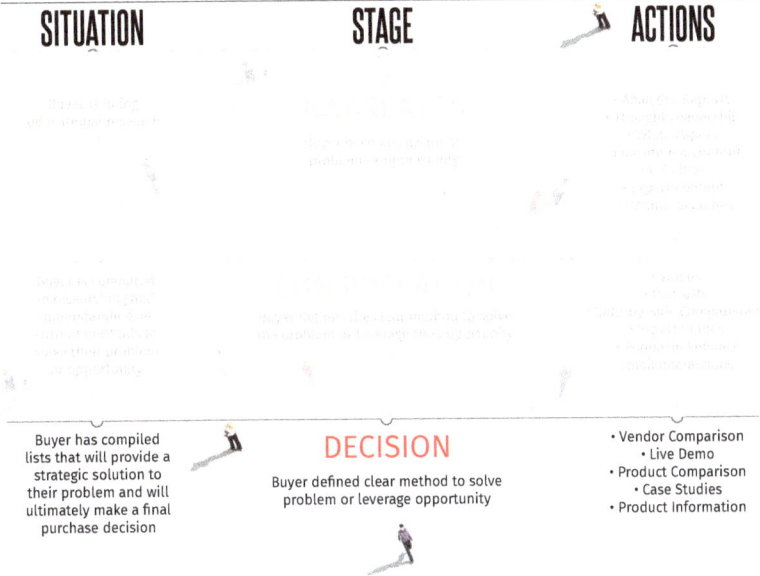

SITUATION	STAGE	ACTIONS
Buyer has compiled lists that will provide a strategic solution to their problem and will ultimately make a final purchase decision	**DECISION** Buyer defined clear method to solve problem or leverage opportunity	• Vendor Comparison • Live Demo • Product Comparison • Case Studies • Product Information

At the decision stage, buyers know what they want and need to understand the key differences between available options. From your perspective, this primarily means the key ways you are different from and better than your competition.

Buyers at this stage want *facts*. At best, the facts are so unadorned with sales talk and extraneous detail that you could fairly and accurately describe them as data. Buyers want to know everything necessary to make a rapid and informed decision. Keep in mind that for B2B sales, your clients could be risking their jobs or businesses on the decision.

---

17   Or not to buy.

They want accuracy, honesty, and personalized recommendations from an expert they trust.

If you've done your job right during the awareness and consideration phases, that trusted expert will be you—unless you derail the process during this last stage, which is easier to do than you might think.

This close to the finish line, buyers can still be turned off by rookie mistakes, like trying to increase the sale by adding extra services that don't solve the problem that brought them to the table. Using the hard sell at the end can lose all the credibility you so carefully built up to this point, as will any surprises, like hidden costs and fees.

Unresponsive sales reps are another huge problem at this stage. Remember: modern buyers are sophisticated and informed. If you take your sweet time getting to their questions *just before the sale*, they will make[18] assumptions about how they'll be treated once you have their money.

WHAT IF THE COMPETITION IS BETTER?

One major question I'm often asked at this point is what to do when the competition has traits, prices, or other features superior to your own. You've set yourself up as a trustworthy adviser, but what if the most honest advice to buyers is to purchase from somebody else?

The best move in these cases is to still give the most honest advice. In many cases, buyers will chose your product anyway because of the relationship you've built. Even if they don't, which vendor do you think they will recommend to their friends? The one they bought from, or the one who gave them honest advice, even though it cost a sale?

Decision-Stage Best Practices

Your content for the decision stage is about helping buyers make a

---

18   Almost certainly justified and accurate.

decision. It should offer all the information they need to make that decision and none of the information they don't need. It is your job to provide that information as completely, understandably, transparently, and neutrally as possible.

- ✓ Focus on the relevant details about your product and comparable products in the industry. This would be the time to provide cost breakdowns, comparison charts, and similar deep details.

- ✓ Use keywords associated with general comparison, as well as those for the industry you serve. Again, include general terms like compare, versus, pros and cons, and benchmarks. "Consumer report" and "consumer review" are also good calls.

- ✓ Ask yourself which qualities you strove for when creating your product and how they differentiate you from the competition.

- ✓ Consider questions other buyers asked you at this stage and how you answered them most successfully.

- ✓ Avoid even appearing to "massage" your numbers or otherwise provide a biased comparison. You've invested too much in earning the buyer's trust to betray it at this point.

- ✓ Provide content containing meaningful apples-to-apples comparisons of specific products, like vendor comparisons, product comparisons, case studies, free trials and downloads, and specific product literature.

Hopefully, the end result of this stage is happy clients buying from you, who are primed to be delighted by the quality of your product and service. Overall, you want to continue increasing your credibility at this stage while showing information that reduces perceived risk on the part of buyers.

The decision stage is your opportunity to get the payoff for your previous investments of time and capital. As with every other stage of the buyer's journey, this will happen if you maintain focus on the relationship and on your role as coach and caring mentor. Though you will make several shifts in the *type* and *tone* of your content at this stage, if you shift your *intent* from relationship to sale, you have a good chance of losing both.

✋ Time To Take Five

FIVE KEY TAKEAWAYS FROM THIS SECTION

- [ ] 1. Marketing without looking at the full funnel is dumb. It's like taking drugs for a symptom without finding a cure.
- [ ] 2. Traditional marketing has the wrong focus.
- [ ] 3. Traditional marketing has the wrong methods.
- [ ] 4. Everything must be trackable if you want to engineer better profits.
- [ ] 5. Do not trust yourself to know what's going on just because many things feel familiar. It all has fundamentally changed.

FIVE THINGS TO DO THIS MONTH

- [ ] 1. Mind-map your content so you can brainstorm and strategize.
- [ ] 2. Map leads to acquisition methods to help you understand what's already working.
- [ ] 3. List the metrics you already use to track your profit engineering results.
- [ ] 4. Diagram your attraction system to help you understand the structure of your marketing.
- [ ] 5. Find out key attraction performance metrics for your industry and company so you know where you stand in the larger picture.

SECTION 2 | CONVERSION

CONVERSION

BUSINESS SCHOOL DEFINITION

A marketing tactic that encourages customers to take specific actions

PROFIT ENGINEERING DEFINITION

The strategy of offering potential clients something of value for their contact information

"

Make certain to measure the quality of leads generated via your conversion offering. A trade show raffle can get a lot of email addresses, but how many are interested in your product and not just the free iGizmo?

PART 1
SCIENTIFIC CONVERSION MANAGEMENT
EXECUTIVE SUMMARY

In this section, we'll discuss:

- Applying the scientific method to lead conversion
- Testing hypotheses in the field

THE SCIENTIFIC METHOD OF LEAD CONVERSION

"Okay," I said. "Time to get nerdy."

"Now?" Carole said. "So up to now we haven't already been nerdy?"

Chuck … um … chuckled.

"Anyway," I said, "let's talk about the scientific method."

"You mean that thing I had to memorize in middle school science?"

"Probably," I said.

"ROY G BIV," said Chuck Jones.

"No," said Carole, "the other thing we had to memorize in middle school science."

"Oh. Which thing was that?"

"The scientific method," I said. "It's a step-by-step method for using math and observation to determine if something you think might be true is, in fact, true."

"And this has something to do with marketing my company?"

"Trust me. It has everything to do with that."

If you're like most people, you remember the concept of the scientific method from middle school science class. Also, if you're like most people, you probably need a review of the specifics.

Well, this method is not just for the lab. It can be applied to your business-development funnels, which enables you to get more leads, focus on qualified leads, and increase sales.

The scientific method is a systematic approach to answering questions about the world. It consists of six steps, each of which will probably feel familiar to you as we walk through them in this chapter.

They won't just feel familiar because you flash back to middle school. A/B testing, which people in your position will have done repeatedly in their careers, runs through the same steps:

- ✓ Observation

- ✓ Question

- ✓ Hypothesis

- ✓ Experiment

- ✓ Analysis

- ✓ Conclusion

Let's start by examining each step in detail and looking at A/B testing through this lens.

The Steps of the Scientific Method

The power of the scientific method is that it offers a template for exploring the universe. It serves as both a guide and a reminder for how to keep what you *want* to be true from getting in the way of finding out what's actually going on. It begins with observing something you want to know more about and ends with a specific, quantified conclusion about that observation.

Observation

Isaac Asimov once wrote, "The most exciting phrase to hear in science is not 'Eureka,' but 'That's funny.'"

The scientific method begins with somebody noticing something about the universe that's odd, important, or challenging. Archimedes noticed that a crown's volume was hard to measure because it had such an odd shape. Salk noticed that the polio virus was both deadly *and* vulnerable to the human immune system. A coder notices that every time somebody right-clicks an icon in his program, the computer crashes.

In all of these examples, the observation inspires the scientist to learn more.

A/B testing begins with the observation that two marketing messages are likely to bring results. This observation inspires profit engineers to find out which brings the *best* results.

Question

The next step is forming a specific question related to the observation. Though it's possible to just randomly apply stimulus to a subject, it's very hard to derive any meaningful conclusions from that.

Instead, scientific (and profit engineering) experimentation demands a question that is as specific as possible:

- ✓ Archimedes asked, "How can I measure the volume of an irregular object?"

- ✓ Salk asked, "How can I keep people from being crippled and dying from the polio virus?"

- ✓ That coder asks, "How can I keep my program from crashing?"

When it comes to A/B testing, the question is always the same: "Will message A or message B produce the strongest response in this media channel?"

Hypothesis

In the hypothesis stage, scientists turn that question into an informed guess. It's a little like the opposite of *Jeopardy*: You ask the question again, this time in the form of a statement.

Archimedes turned his question into the statement, "I can measure the volume of an irregular object by submerging it in water and measuring the volume of the water it displaces."

Jonas Salk's hypothesis was, "I can stimulate immunity to the polio virus by vaccinating subjects with a small amount of the virus itself."

That coder's hypothesis is, "I can keep my program from crashing by changing lines 101 to 103 of my code."

In A/B testing, you fudge things a little with a hypothesis that keeps you from favoring one or the other: "Either message A or message B will perform significantly better than the other, thus giving us a clear path for our marketing."

Experiment

This is the fun part of science, the part where people get to tinker with the source code of the universe and see what's what. It's also the most complex and the easiest to screw up.

In this stage, scientists set up situations in which they can test the hypothesis and prove or disprove it. In the next chapter, we'll look deeply at the elements of a good experiment.

Archimedes submerged a crown in the bath, measured the volume of water it displaced, and then measured its volume the "old-fashioned way." Then he did the same with a variety of other objects.

Salk vaccinated subjects with his vaccine, then observed whether they were immune to polio. This was the final step after multiple iterations of experiments in petri dishes and on test animals.

That coder changes lines 101 to 103 of his program, then runs it again and clicks on that icon.

With A/B testing, profit engineers make a limited run of *both* marketing messages and compare the results.

Analysis

The second-to-last stage of the scientific method is looking at the results of the experiment to see what it tells you about your hypothesis.

Archimedes compared the results of submersion and regular measurement for each object he tried to see if they matched.

Salk tracked how many test subjects contracted polio after being vaccinated, compared to subjects who had not received the vaccine.

The coder runs the program again, clicks on the icon, and sees if the computer still crashes.

The profit engineer looks at how many leads message A got and how many leads were received from message B.

Conclusion

This part is why the scientific method is so powerful. By formulating a highly specific hypothesis, then testing it with a careful experiment and analyzing the results, a scientist is led to a specific (and hopefully irrefutable) conclusion. Because the method is so exacting, the scientist should only be able to draw a single conclusion about the hypothesis once the data comes in.

In Archimedes's case, *every single measurement* matched. If even one of the objects had showed water displacement with a different volume than measurement and math, his hypothesis would have been disproven.

Salk was able to conclude that his vaccine was effective by the finding that a significantly lower number of vaccinated people contracted polio under the same conditions as those without the vaccine.

The coder knows whether his changes fixed the program by whether it still crashes when right-clicking the icon.

In A/B testing, you can tell which message works best by which produces the most positive response.

The Scientific Method and Conversion Management

You will use the scientific method in A/B testing and other profit-engineering applications by asking and answering questions about which steps in your sales funnel are working well. Some sample questions you'll need to investigate by experiment include:

✓ What do our potential clients value?

✓ What messaging resonates with them?

✓ What are the fundamental pains of our potential customers?

✓ What are they looking for to help them solve their problems?

✓ Is there a loss leader opportunity to start the conversation and build trust?

Just as in scientific exploration, some of those questions are closed-ended yes/no or A/B questions. Others are more open, "I wonder what happens when I …" questions.

Both are valid types of questions. The former is more useful for forming a plan of action. The latter are best for initial exploration to help you create an actual hypothesis.

As an engineer, profit or otherwise, active experimentation and careful recording of results is part of your job. In the next chapter, we'll look at how to devise an effective experiment that gives you the most accurate possible results about what's working and not working in your conversion tactics.

CHAPTER 11
TESTING HYPOTHESES

"Okay," Chuck said. "That rings a bell. How do we get started?"

"Well, the order is pretty clear. It's set up that way on purpose," Carole said. Chuck gave her a dirty look, but nodded.

"The good news is that a lot of the steps are the same for any profit engineering effort," I said. "The trickiest part is the hypothesis-testing phase."

"That's the actual experiment, right?" Carole said.

"Yep."

"And what's tricky about it?"

"Making sure you set up the experiment so you measure what you think you're measuring."

"What?"

"Ever hear that old joke about how a scientist looked at traffic patterns and decided that people could get to and from work faster if we all changed the work day to noon to eight?"

"No. How's it go?"

"He'd noticed that traffic got bad at nine and at five, so he figured people should commute at other times."

"Ohhhh," said Carole.

"Gotcha," said Chuck

"So here's how we avoid making that kind of mistake."

Of the stages in the scientific method, experimentation is the most complex, intimidating, and easy to mess up. It's also where the most important parts of science happen. Every time you read articles with contradictory scientific findings, you're usually looking at a poorly conducted experiment.

Every time somebody makes a disastrously wrong call about marketing and conversion, you're either looking at a poorly conducted experiment[19] or (much more often) no experiment at all.

So here's how to conduct your conversion experiments correctly.

Elementary, My Dear Watson

All experiments consist of a handful of carefully controlled elements. If your exploration into your conversion methods includes careful construction of each of these, it should yield good results. If an element is missing in your consideration or is not tightly controlled, your conclusions will be questionable. And decisions based on questionable conclusions often yield poor results.

Hypothesis

An experiment is only as good as its hypothesis, a statement or question that defines the purpose of the experiment. Operating without one is like going on a cruise without a destination. Even with excellent maps and a high-quality boat, you'll get *somewhere* … but you might not necessarily end up where you want to go.

The good news about hypotheses for profit engineering is that you'll be able to use the same ones over and over again. You'll just slot in different variables and subjects.

For example, in an A/B test, your hypothesis could be, "Which of these options generates the most leads over one week?" One time "these options" might be two different Facebook ads. The next, "these options" might be two banner ads. A third time, it might be a pair of titles for your value-added e-book.

---

19   Or poorly conducted science journalism, but that's a whole different story.

Variables

Variables are the factors in an experiment that you change and compare to one another—the "moving parts" of the machine. It's important to limit the number of active variables in any experiment; otherwise, you might be measuring things that are different from what you're trying to figure out.

When discussing variables, there are two kinds you need to pay close attention to.

✓ ***Control variable.*** This is something you measure without making any changes so you can be sure that whatever you're doing in your experiment has a meaningful effect. In medical experiments, the control variable is often a placebo. Test subjects are given a sugar pill and told it's medicine to see what impact nothing at all has on them. This is then compared to the impact of the medical treatment to make sure it's worth doing.

✓ ***Confounding variables.*** These are things that impact a test subject unintentionally, in ways that might confuse you when you analyze your data. For example, because of the time rush hour happens in most cities, an uninformed researcher might conclude that dusk and dawn *cause* heavy traffic. The fact that rush hour often happens at sunrise and sunset is a confounding variable.

It's your job to construct your profit engineering experiment to include one (and only one) control variable and to avoid or understand confounding variables as much as possible.

With an A/B test, your control variable is your baseline number of website hits or similar performance metrics. If those don't change while running your tests, you can conclude that neither of your marketing options are performing well enough to use.

The calendar is an example of a confounding variable for A/B testing. If you run a sports betting website and run test A the week before the Super Bowl and test B the week after, test A will overwhelmingly outperform test B. But that won't be because test A was the better piece of marketing.

Metrics

Metrics are the numbers you compare when looking at the results of an experiment. It's *possible* to carry out an experiment and get meaningful results without specific, empirical metrics, but it's really hard.

The good news is that modern marketing software (more on that in a bit) automatically generates *tons* of metrics for you to analyze. A few of the most common and important are:

✓ The number of impressions a given tactic generates

✓ The conversion rate of a given tactic

✓ The ROI for a given marketing strategy

✓ Your *P-value*: your confidence level that the numbers you're looking at actually measure what you're trying to measure

In A/B testing, your metric will be some measure of how well people respond to each of the two messages you're testing against one another. If you're comparing two emails, your metric would be the number of click-throughs generated by each.

One final note on metrics: pay attention to *significance*. It's impossible to cut out every possible confounding variable from your experiment because you're conducting it in the real world. Any difference in your results that amounts to less than 5 percent of the total probably shows that your two tests aren't significantly different or that you're comparing them using the wrong metric.

Why Test Hypotheses?

Setting up, conducting, measuring, and analyzing profit engineering experiments is *hard*. So why bother?

You bother because this kind of tight observation, measurement, and analysis allows you to make the small course corrections that add up to getting where you want to be as quickly as you can.

Keep in mind that profit growth happens at several different points, and a gain at each point can mean huge gains in your overall income.

Testing hypotheses helps you determine the best places to aim for those gains.

For example, say you have a 1 percent response rate on a given ad campaign and a 10 percent conversion rate on those responses. Adding 1 percent to that conversion rate improves your sales by 1 percent.

But adding 1 percent to that response rate *doubles the number of responses*, increasing your sales by 100 percent.

Testing hypotheses helps you see those opportunities and act on them.

Modern technology makes this possible today in ways that never before were even imaginable. And if it's possible to grow your business by reliably using careful experimentation coupled with unbiased analysis, then it's your responsibility to do exactly that.

This is where the engineering and scientific approach really begins to diverge—at least in language—from the traditional way of marketing for businesses. But now you understand *how* the scientific method guides powerful profit engineering. You also understand *which* steps in the scientific method are most effective in analyzing your marketing efforts. You understand *what* you must change, measure, and analyze to put the right changes in the right places and maximize your marketing return.

PART 2
YOUR WEBSITE
EXECUTIVE SUMMARY

In this section, we'll discuss:

- Why your website is the unsung hero of your lead conversion
- The best offers and calls to action to include on your site
- Establishing thought leadership using your website and web presence

CHAPTER 12
OFFERS AND CALLS TO ACTION

"Now let me tell you about generating leads."

"Come on," Chuck said. *"I've been in business for two decades. I know about generating leads."*

"You also know about marketing, advertising, and social media—but we've already established how what you knew has changed faster than a teenager's favorite band."

"Uh, okay. Fair enough."

"This is one place where digital marketing truly shines. If you do it right, you'll reach more leads for less money than you ever did using traditional marketing methods. The internet automates the first steps while also allowing a degree of tight targeting never before possible."

"If I do it right?"

"Yep. If you do it right."

"How do I do it right?"

"Well …"

The goal and general process of lead generation haven't changed since leads for businesses became a thing. Since the internet *changed everything*, though, many of the key components of lead generation hardly resemble the tools used during the twentieth century.

This is true of offers and calls to action (CTAs), the two most important aspects of your website lead generation engine. Both have existed since the earliest days of marketing, often surrounded by words like "Act Now!" and "Call Today" and "Free Gift!"

Modern consumers are wary of such sales-speak, but still want the free gift and are willing to act now if the gift gives sufficient value ... and if you make acting simple enough.

Your website conversion system will include three key elements:

✓ **Lead generation page**: the web page where visitors land when they follow a link or enter a URL you advertise. This is different from your home page. As we'll see, the most effective websites have multiple lead generation pages, each with a different purpose.

✓ **Offer**: content or something else of value, offered in the copy on a lead generation page. The offer both *demonstrates your expertise* and *elicits* by informing the reader in the form of clicking through.

✓ **Call to action (CTA)**: a clearly labeled instruction that tells casual readers what to do if they want to get more deeply involved with your content, website, or company. This element is the heart of automated lead generation and, if done right, will be the most effective salesperson on your team.

These features of digital lead generation form the core of every aspect of your website and other online content. Memorize them. Love them. Live them. Sleep with them.[20] Here's how to make each as effective as possible.

Lead Generation Page

This item wasn't listed in the chapter title because it's more of a home to

---

20   In your head.

the important elements than an element unto itself. But it's as vital to this process as a plate is to a gourmet meal.

A lead generation page is where visitors first arrive after clicking a link from search, advertising, or other awareness-stage efforts. It's the first significant contact you have with casually interested readers, and its job is to move those readers from casual interest to legitimate leads.

Do not confuse your lead generation page with your home page. Some[21] websites have a home page that is also a lead generation page, but most companies will have several lead generation pages, each tuned to a different product or client profile. One of these may or may not *also* be the site's home page.

When setting up a lead generation page, consider these best practices:

✓ **More is better**. Multiple pages tied to different questions, buyer types, and products are more likely to "hook" casual readers than a single one-size-fits-all page.

✓ **Communicate clearly**. Express what readers can get from that page and how they can get further information. This is not the place for jargon or your best grammar-school essay skills. Stay simple, to the point, and easy to *want* to read.

✓ **Grab attention**. Do things that demand notice early and often. Consumers land on your lead generation page *looking for a reason to navigate away*. You have less than five seconds to give them a reason to stay, and only one hundred to two hundred words to convince them to stay.

✓ **Reduce anxiety.** This is how you begin to establish your role as an adviser. Readers don't come to you without a problem they hope you will solve. They're anxious about both the problem itself and the experience they will have with the company they hire to solve it. Use offers, phrasing, and the beginnings of your mentor-student relationship to put both of those anxieties at ease.

---

21 Usually simpler.

✓ **Create urgency**. Use psychological cues like the bandwagon effect, limited quantities, hyperbolic discounting, and loss-aversion bias to get readers to click your CTA *now*.

While you're at it, avoid several of the most common rookie mistakes I've encountered on otherwise well-built web pages.

Resist the temptation to "build up" to a call to action. The top of your lead generation page *must* grab readers' attention and create an emotional attachment to you and your online content.

Never skimp on design. Just as you keep your lobby clean and your staff looking professional, your lead generation pages must be sharp and easy to navigate. A study from Stanford University found that unprofessional lead generation pages resulted almost universally in high bounce rates and left readers with a bad impression of the business overall.

Don't ask for too much information. The more fields you ask readers to fill out, the less likely people are to fill out the form and complete the signup. You can always gather additional information later in the journey, after you've developed a relationship you can leverage.

Your Offer

Your offer is the bait on your lead generation hook: content or another item of value, in exchange for which a visitor will give you their contact information.

Do not confuse an offer with a link to further marketing collateral or one of those little panes encouraging readers to sign up for your newsletter. Neither of those provide sufficient value to turn viewers into subscribers. An offer must be worth more than that, presenting the casual viewer with "an offer she can't refuse."

Consider these pro tips for offer design:

✓ **Begin with the customer in mind**. Craft your specific offers to specific buyer profiles. This includes demographics, positions within your typical business client, specific points in the buyer's journey, regional location, and any other detail of your ideal client that might impact what offers value and what does not.

✓ **Offer a wide selection.** What's absolutely compelling to one high-value lead might be of no use to another. Multiple offers targeted to different types of buyers far outperform a single one-size-fits-all attempt.

✓ **Test and track.** Check the metrics of all offers regularly to see which performs best and which traits grab the most attention. Consistently tweak, test, and fine-tune all your offers until each is generating enough leads to justify the resources you put into it.

✓ **Give massive value.** Each offer should give away knowledge or a service for which people would be willing to pay you cash. You want page visitors to see your offer as a golden opportunity, not a favor you're asking them to do for you.

The biggest and most common rookie mistake I see is hiding all the best content behind a lead capture offer. In this situation, only subscribers can see your content. Since the purpose of the content is to attract subscribers, this does very little for you. Your strongest marketing material—like product descriptions, customer case studies, and white papers—should be available for *all to see*. Leave plenty of that content, plus your first-stage blog posts, open and available, and imply[22] that there's even better stuff on the other side of the call to action.

A second common error is to keep the offers secret by confining them to forms available from your lead generation pages. Mention all offers early and often via your social media feeds, pay-per-click campaigns, even your outbound marketing efforts. The more people who learn about your offer, the more qualified leads will give you their contact information.

Your Call to Action (CTA)

Your CTA is an image that drives readers to click-through to your offer or other online content. It's there so visitors to your site know what to do next once you've successfully piqued their interest.

---

22 With honesty.

You'll notice I said the CTA is an *image*. Linked text in bold face, embedded at the bottom of your content, does not cut it. CTA buttons result in 200 percent higher click-throughs than text. Your CTA should be one of the most visible elements on the page. Do not skimp on its quality or placement.

Other top-level pro tips for your CTA include:

✓ **Keep it simple, sunshine.** Your CTA should be clean and unclut-tered, containing just one idea, with simple instructions on how to execute that idea.

✓ **What's in it for them?** Clearly state the benefits of answering your call in terms your clients/industry/tribe can understand.

✓ **Begin with conversion in mind.** Make your CTA part of a clearly defined step-by-step journey toward conversion. Depending on the page, this could be visitor-to-lead, lead-to-qualified-lead, or qualified-lead-to-sale.

✓ **Two CTAs enter, one CTA leaves.** Run A/B testing on your site, for your mailing list, and via PPC runs to determine what messag-ing and images create the best results. Make real-time changes and adjustments informed by those tests.

✓ **Map the stages** of the buyer's journey so all visitors have some-thing specific to do after reading the high-value content on any page they visit.

As with your landing page, you shouldn't limit yourself to a single CTA. You should begin and end each page with a CTA. The call above the fold is there to grab readers' attention in a hurry or those who are already at a later stage in the buyer's journey. The one at the end capi-talizes on the value received by somebody who has just read the whole page. While you're at it, avoid the trap of matching the CTA's color to the page's visual design. Do everything to make it "pop." High contrast gets attention, and attention gets click-throughs.

CHAPTER 13

ESTABLISHING THOUGHT LEADERSHIP

"So that's how you lead people to your website and, thus, to your company."

"Okay," Chuck said. "I see how that works."

"Want to learn about something even cooler?"

"Why, yes, Ryan. Yes, I do."

"There's another process that gets people to look for your company on their own. They'll come to your website without any prompting at all."

"And this is where you tell me I can have it for three payments of $19.95?"

"Naw. I'll tell you about thought leadership for free."

"Thought leadership isn't new."

"No, but just like the buyer's journey, how you get there sure is."

Some things never change. Even before mass communication, a highly visible and wealthy dilettante was taken more seriously than a reclusive expert. During the twentieth century, well-meaning amateurs and dedicated charlatans could tour TV talk shows and radio programs to make a mint selling their dubious advice, while true experts without media savvy wallowed in obscurity.

New technologies haven't changed this basic fact of human nature, but they have changed what you can do about it.

Back then, you had to rely on others' broadcast platforms to become a well-known leader in your area of expertise. Now, it's up to you to do it via your blogs, social media platforms, and online discussion communities. It's never been more important to create a powerful online presence:

The degree to which you establish thought leadership in your area of expertise is the degree to which your inbound marketing is likely to succeed.

A Tale of Two "Experts"

To illustrate the importance of online thought leadership, take the example of two hypothetical people working in banking compliance services.

1. Bob has a master's degree in economics and fifteen years of experience in banking, five of those as the chief compliance officer for a bank. He speaks at banking conferences and gives two lectures each year for FBI training in their bank fraud division. He's not active on social media, and his blog is about his hobbies: model trains and science fiction movies.

2. Jen has a bachelor's degree in creative writing. Just out of college, she got a job writing the blog for a banking compliance consulting company. Her contract stipulated that she engage on social media around her posts and that she get the byline on the blog. She really wants to write the great American novel. Meanwhile, blogging for the consulting firm pays her bills.

As far as the internet is concerned, Jen is a far more authoritative expert on banking compliance than Bob because Jen has established an online presence as an expert and is a thought leader in the banking compliance community.

It ain't fair, and it ain't right. But "fair" and "right" aren't the same as "true."

The degree to which you establish thought leadership in your area of expertise is the degree to which your inbound marketing is likely to succeed, and thought leadership has little to do with how qualified you are to lead.

The good news is that experts like you can start establishing themselves as thought leaders right now. Today. Using tools you likely already have up and running.

The bad news is that the playing field is mighty crowded.

THOUGHT LEADERSHIP COMPETITION

31%

There are 31% more bloggers active today than there were in 2012 and there were a lot of bloggers in 2012

40%

Nearly 40% of US companies use blogs for marketing purposes

Every B2B topic, even niche topics, already has at least one go-to named expert for its specialty. However, this doesn't mean you can't establish yourself as a thought leader for what you do. It just means you'll have to work hard—and smart—to get yourself there. You're a successful businessperson already, so you know all about working hard.

Here is our recommended path for working smart:

✓ *Focus your content* using keyword research to identify not just the most popular search terms related to your business but the terms that will give you the most impact for your effort.

✓ *Build calls to action* with a core objective into your content so visitors are led inexorably toward becoming interested and qualified leads (or at least impressed advocates for your page).

✓ *Monitor news and social media* for high-profile topics that you can turn into frequently shared, relevant, and evergreen content.

✓ *Systematize your content generation* to make your online content and inbound marketing a prioritized initiative in your business, not the afterthought that more than 30% of your competition thinks it is.

✓ *Double-dip on all of your content* by turning blog posts into sections of an e-book, expanding conversations into webinars, and otherwise leveraging what you build in as many ways as possible.

✓ *Have quality of quantity blogs* not only well but with intent. Divide your time equally between writing your content and sharing that content in relevant social media spaces like Google Plus and LinkedIn.

✓ *Blog with intent.* Don't spend any time writing a blog post that isn't a defined part of your overall marketing strategy. Do the research to identify the best keywords, social media strategies, and images to go with it.

It's Worth Every Hour You Put into It

In the twenty-first–century marketing battleground, your thought leadership position is one of the most powerful tools available for dominating your market. The time you spend on this pays off in ways that few other investments of your resources can.

Take a look at some of the numbers behind this statement:

THOUGHT LEADERSHIP FACTS

46%
46% of people read blogs more than once a day.

13X
Marketers who have prioritized blogging are 13x more likely to enjoy positive ROI.

84%
84% of inbound marketers - compared to only 9% of outbound marketers - cite organic sources (blogging, SEO, social media) as rising in importance.

82%
82% of marketers who blog daily acquired customers using their blog, as opposed to 57% of marketers who blog monthly, which by itself is still an impressive result.

79%
79% of companies that have a blog, report a positive ROI for inbound marketing in 2013.

Of course, it's not just about getting your words out and attracting attention. You need systems in place for what to do when that attention arrives in the form of interested leads.

Read on to learn the exciting things the twenty-first century has in store for you about that.

🖐 Time To Take Five

FIVE KEY TAKEAWAYS FROM THIS SECTION

- [ ] 1. Conversion is as important as, if not more important than, attraction.
- [ ] 2. Applying the scientific method to your conversion metrics drastically improves your yield.
- [ ] 3. Knowing *where* to improve your conversion pipeline is as important as knowing *how*.
- [ ] 4. Your website is the hub of everything you do online.
- [ ] 5. Establishing thought leadership can improve your conversion in a myriad of ways.

FIVE THINGS TO DO THIS MONTH

- [ ] 1. Find out your conversion rate for each part of your pipeline.
- [ ] 2. Ask clients and potential leads how much value they perceive in your offer.
- [ ] 3. Find out if a new viewer can find the CTA on your page within five seconds of first glance.
- [ ] 4. Try a Facebook A/B test for your offers and track the results.
- [ ] 5. Catalog all the credibility cues on your website and in your value added content.

SECTION 3 | CLOSING

CLOSING

BUSINESS SCHOOL DEFINITION

The activity or business of selling products or services

PROFIT ENGINEERING DEFINITION

A relationship process where you aim to solve a potential client's problems through education, question-oriented problem-solving, and setting up a win-win scenario for both of you

"

Always be closing" may be a great tagline, but it is dead wrong. 828 sales carries risks for purchasers, and you must be a trusted mentor if you want to create the right relationship for ongoing sales.

PART 1
THE NATURE OF NURTURING LEADS
EXECUTIVE SUMMARY

In this section, we'll discuss:

- How nurturing leads to closure has changed with new technologies and client attitudes
- Two key forms of marketing automation
- Technological retooling for your sales pipeline

CHAPTER 14
ZEN AND THE ART OF LEAD NURTURING

"Okay," I said. "It's time to talk about lead nurturing."

Carole smiled. "You keep using that word. I do not think it means what I think it means."

"That's probably so, but why don't you tell me what you think it means?"

Chuck stepped in, saying, "It's like raising a child. Leads start unready to buy. You nurture leads, raise them, and teach them what they need to know until they're ready to become clients."

"Yup," I said.

"Excellent," said Carole. "So we can go home now?"

"Only if you want to lose leads."

"Go on."

"As you say, lead nurturing has been a thing for a long time, but twenty-first–century lead nurturing needs an automated system for qualifying, grooming, and educating potential buyers. It's a whole different department that's as necessary as sales and production."

"And you're going to tell me how that works?"

"As you wish."

"All men[23] are created equal" … but some leads are more equal than others. Up to 75 percent of your incoming leads will not be worth the time you'll spend following up on them. They're not seriously interested, or they're interested but can't afford you, or they're not ready or authorized to make a buying decision.

That doesn't mean you should ignore that 75 percent. More on that later, but let's start with how to separate qualified and serious buyers from the rest of the pack.

What Are Qualified Leads?

Qualified leads are worth all the sales attention your resources allow. The trick is figuring out which leads are actually qualified. Our research department has identified five key questions to ask of incoming leads that prequalifies them early in your sales process.

- ✓ *Is this person the decision-maker for the company?* If you're not talking to somebody capable of giving a yes, you'll only ever get a no. Either establish contact with the decision-maker or politely educate the minion so you'll have an advocate in that camp.

- ✓ *Are they happy with their current solution to the problem they have?* If they are, your sales will take much more effort, often more than would be cost-effective. Your job with these leads is to slowly but inexorably feed them information to make them progressively less happy with what they're doing now.

- ✓ *Are they able to switch to what you offer?* Contracts, family ties, and strategic alliances can all bind a company to a solution they're not entirely happy with … but all of those situations can end in time. Your lead-nurturing system lets them know you're there, without acting like a poacher.

- ✓ *Can they afford what you sell?* And are they willing to pay it? A *no* here makes the deal a nonstarter … for now. They might be able to later, and they probably know somebody who can.

---

23 And women.

✓ *Is your solution honestly better that what they're currently doing?* Remember the part about being an honest and helpful adviser and not a sales flack? If you can't make the lead's life better, never make money off making it worse. That kind of honesty means the lead will recommend you to people who you can help.

Anybody who answers yes to all five questions goes on your hot list of leads, so living human sales representatives can touch base with them regularly. All others go into your "drip system" to keep you on their minds until they can give the five yeses you need for a fully qualified buyer.

Automated Lead Nurturing via Your Drip System

Automated lead nurturing offers you the best of both worlds. You don't waste your time on people who aren't ready to be qualified leads, but you don't lose their potential.

Multiple studies have found that 50 percent of B2B sales go to vendors who respond first. Automated lead nurturing can respond within seconds, no matter what time of day leads express interest.

A robust lead-nurturing system also gets 400 percent to 1000 percent the response rate of single email blasts, making it one of the most effective marketing initiatives your business can adopt. Further, nurtured leads make 47 percent larger purchases than non-nurtured leads.

Segmented communications[24] get 50 percent more click-throughs than generic email programs. Run all those numbers together, and you can see the massive potential of a well-designed lead-nurturing system.

But the key is a *well-designed* system. The types of emails that are useful for that system are as varied as the types of businesses in the world and the types of potential buyers. That said, they do fall into a few broad categories that work well in almost any lead-nurturing campaign.

---

24   Communications sent to a subset of your lead list, based on what you know about those leads.

✓ Educational emails that offer direct information or links to genuinely helpful white papers, blog articles, webinars, videos and other resources

✓ Promotional content that informs readers about your product in a way that still feels valuable and current

✓ Best practices notes that give a little taste of what you can do, by offering the baseline value of your services for free.

✓ Making emails feel like personal messages directly to them, rather than a generic blast.

✓ Demos or trial offers where readers can click through to get a free, time-sensitive sample of what you offer.

✓ Personal emails keyed to information your campaign has gathered that invites readers to ask specific questions of real people.

You are probably already on a dozen or more lead-nurturing email systems right now. Over the next week, open a few more than you usually do, and see how many fall into one of the above conceptual buckets. Like alcohol and oil changes, they're popular because they work.

But How Do I Make Them Work?

I've seen a lot of bad automated lead nurturing over the past decade, but I've seen and built a lot of good ones too. The best share a handful of common traits.

They divide and conquer. A smart email nurturing program puts the education and qualification portions of the sales discussion in the hands of marketing departments. This lets sales focus solely on the most interested and qualified leads and puts specialists in charge of converting casual inquiries.

They provide massive value. The average business worker opens maybe 10 percent of the lead-nurturing emails they receive each day. This is because they don't trust them to be worth the two minutes it takes to open and skim them. A *working* lead-nurturing system provides emails readers can't wait to open. One of the best examples of this that's operating today is Tim Ferris's *5-Bullet Friday* newsletter. It arrives weekly, promises to be short, fulfills that promise, and directly delivers on-point information of interest to the people who might buy his books.

They analyze, recalibrate, and try again. This analysis begins with knowing your industry: the average open rates, click-through rates, subscription rates, and similar basic rates for what you offer. Compare the results for each email sent against both industry averages and performance from other content within your system. There is no other way to accurately assess how valuable your lead-nurturing system is.

They focus energy on the title. Titles and subtitles are visible before the email gets opened. When these pop, your email gets opened. If not, they don't. The most brilliant and effective email does you no good if it goes directly into the spam box.

They are timed carefully. Different client bases have different "golden hours" when decision-makers are (a) online and (b) not too busy to read your email. Different segments of your mailing list will be in different time zones, thus shifting when their golden hours are, relative to your location. Plan your email schedule accordingly to maximize who opens them.

One last thing about lead nurturing: It's a good idea to touch on other areas for highly qualified leads. Handwritten cards. LinkedIn connections. Grab a beer. Multiple points of contact for high-valued leads.

Now, go nurture those leads.

CHAPTER 15

INFO, INFO, EVERYWHERE

"We're already setting you up to get a flood of requests, leads, and new business."

"I should hope so. That's rather the point," Chuck said.

"Are you ready for it?"

"I should hope so. That's rather the point," Carole said.

"But are you really ready for it?"

"I suspect you're building to something," Chuck pointed out.

"You're right. We've found that a lot of our clients find themselves flooded with information and requests for information once we get the profit engineering process fully online."

"I should hope so ..." Chuck began.

"Yes, that's the point. But there's rarely a faster business-killer than getting the word out and not being ready for it. "

"True," Chuck said. He nodded like he was remembering something painful.

"So you need to get ready for it."

"How do we do that?"

"I'm not the world's leading expert on that, but I've had enough experience to point you to where you should look and to some of the tools that best help solve the problem."

Information is the fuel that your business runs on, and setting up systematic profit engineering runs it on high-octane gas. But only if you manage the information well.

If you're a sole proprietor or solopreneur, it's possible to keep all that information in your head or in a personal planner, but as a business grows, the information load becomes overwhelming. Even if it's not too much for an individual to manage, the departure of that individual from the company can become a crippling blow. And if it's *you* managing all that information, you never get to go on vacation.

Knowledge management systems are what you use to corral knowledge in a way that eliminates memory lapses, gives access to the people who need it when they need it, and prevents any one individual from becoming vital to the company's success.

Each company has three areas of knowledge management:

✓ Knowledge management hub

✓ Customer relationship management

✓ Project management

Let's look at these in turn. We'll talk about what they are, why they matter, and the best tools I know about to host each one.

Knowledge Management

Knowledge management (KM) is the long-term memory of the company. If you're a graphic designer working out of a home office for two to four clients at a time, it's pretty easy to keep all the parts of the business operations in your head or on a pile of note cards.

But go up a level to a small team of designers with a dozen clients, and you need to start writing things down. Other things become factors that weren't factors when it was a smaller situation. A (very) incomplete list of the knowledge such a company needs to keep, store, and have access to would include:

✓ Best practices for core competencies

✓ Customer and project sequences

✓ 5,000-foot-view client folders

✓ HR procedures

✓ Employee data

✓ Employee handbook

✓ Emergency procedures

✓ Instructions for complex company equipment

✓ Training manuals

These documents don't just help with day-to-day operations. They also eliminate the possibility of a single point of failure. Any company with an "ask Bob" knowledge-management system is in serious trouble if Bob gets hit by a bus.

When I think of twentieth-century knowledge management, I think of McDonald's. If you've ever been in the manager's office of any Mickey Dee's, you remember the shelf of binders.

That shelf had everything. There was a binder of checklists for hiring. One with checklists for firing. One for closing. One for opening. One for checking food quality. One for everything.

And they were there, neatly branded and labeled, within arm's reach of managers on duty.

That's knowledge management.

The same sort of comprehensive system is common (and necessary) today, but the best ones are online. Internal wikis, Zendesk, and Confluence are three that I recommend to my clients as often as they'll listen to me.

Best Practices

There's no "One True Knowledge-Management System to Rule Them All," but I've seen a lot of success and failure when it comes to putting one together. The successful knowledge-management systems have all shared a handful of traits.

Successful knowledge-management systems:
Empower people to become active by demonstrably making everybody's job easier. If this is clear and true, 20 to 40 percent of your team will get crazy-excited about it and want to contribute. That contribution will snowball into a general adoption of the system.

Give it an engaging name. This is weird but completely true and reliable. If you name your knowledge-management system the "company wiki," you won't have buy-in. But if you name it "HAL" or "the Almighty Know-It-All," then people will use it and refer to it by name. They'll even start anthropomorphizing it and giving it nicknames. When your team starts cussing *at* your KM hub instead of *about* it, that's a sign you've done this part correctly.

Integrate it into your corporate culture. Too often, somebody sets up a great KM system but nobody adopts, uses, or updates it. That's wasted time. Put a link to it where employees live online to make access easy and intuitive. When starting out, hold contests to make engagement fun. Some clients even put Easter eggs in the KM system to encourage general engagement and exploration.

Document how people are supposed to interact with the system, and encourage compliance. If your knowledge management is hard to use or unpopular, nobody is going to use it. Instead, make *learning* the system so easy that everybody takes the time, and nobody tells the new guy to ignore it and "just ask Bob."

Customer-Relationship Management

Customer-relationship management (CRM) is not a new concept. Since long before software was a thing, smart sales teams had pen-and-paper organization and systems that tracked the progress of various leads and the performance of various initiatives and team members. *CRM software* takes that concept and leverages the power of the digital age to make it a far more powerful beast.

Let's look at the who, what, when, why, and how of CRM software.

What Is CRM?

In some crowds, *CRM* is as much a meaningless buzzword as *SEO*—and it has about the same number of unscrupulous businesspeople offering useless "solutions" surrounding those three letters.

At its best, customer-management software is a suite of digital trackers tied to tasks for automated systems and human sales team members. The good ones accomplish a set of specific tasks that are core to successful sales and customer satisfaction while simultaneously enabling companies to track their sales pipeline in real time.

Who Uses CRM?

This question requires two different answers, depending on what you mean by "who."

If "who" refers to people, both your sales and management teams will use CRM. For the sales team, the info from your CRM software is the lifeblood from which all of their leads, customer details, and data flow. Management uses it to better direct the sales team and to better manage the company's financials.

If "who" refers to companies, simple CRM software is available, even for micropreneurial and home-based ventures. Complex, top-shelf, six-figure-a-year packages are available for multinational corporations, and something appropriate exists for every size of business in between.

When Does CRM Apply?

It comes into play during the second half of the buyer's journey, after interested consumers become qualified leads. It picks up the baton from marketing automation and provides tools that let your sales team give each lead laser-focused attention.

It's also a constant presence in the sales department's "back room." There, it compiles metrics to both help you fine-tune your sales approach and make more accurate sales and revenue predictions for coming quarters.

Finally, CRM also applies to long-term customer relationships. It's how you keep track of your growing list of clients so you can keep them, check in with them, identify upsell opportunities, and generally leverage that list as systematically and well as you do your list of potential buyers.

Why Use CRM?

Customer-relationship management has always been about tracking the progress of clients through the buyer's journey and giving your sales team quick access to vital details, ranging from a lead's potential budget to the birthday of that long-term client's favorite daughter.[25]

Digital-age CRM software takes that basic functionality and turns it up to eleven. A few of the most important benefits include:

✓ Automated reminders and alerts when leads are ready for contact

✓ An integrated data dashboard that collates different aspects of leads and campaign

✓ Easy performance metrics, analyzed from multiple angles and available in real time

✓ Customer data available instantly from anywhere, even offline

✓ Using sales data to combine the tasks of creating a sales pipeline with accurate sales forecasting

✓ Establishing institutional memory in your sales force, so lost team members don't mean lost leads

✓ Improved customer service via seamless tracking of details

How to Best Leverage CRM

Like so many of even the best tools, CRM is only as good as the skill of the person using it and how well the system was set up. You're not an expert on CRM (otherwise, you wouldn't need to be reading this), but you can act like one by following just a few of these best practices:

Track engagement carefully. Your CRM software will keep track of

---

25 We're not supposed to have favorites, but everybody does. And your job is to know which is your client's.

what messages get opened, who does the opening, and what actions readers take. It will tell you which of your value-added content gets downloaded most often, by whom and at what times. Track all of these numbers, looking for the patterns that will help you discover your most effective marketing possibilities.

Personalize all engagement. Don't take the lazy road and spray out marketing messages without first names or other personal details. Leave space in everything you send out to include names and/or titles, geographic information, or references to previous material with which you know readers have interacted. This is the age of connected and engaged marketing. Live in it.

Make lead scoring part of your culture. Lead scoring tells you, within a fair degree of accuracy, how ready somebody is to make a buy. Include these scores in all your communications, decision-making, and prioritization of new leads. Train your sales team on what numbers have to exist for an efficient and effective close to happen. Make watching lead scores as valued as watching sales statistics.

Go deep, not wide. The epic superpower of CRM is that it gives you lots of specific information about individual leads. You can use this to craft the ultimate version of target-specific marketing. Don't broadcast a tangential message to one hundred thousand. Don't even broadcast a reasonably specific message to fifty thousand. Instead, you'll drop a bomb on a thousand leads at the exact time they're perfectly ready to receive it.

Include existing clients. This rookie mistake is as old as business, I think: focusing all your energy on *new* clients while largely ignoring those you already have. Good CRM usage keeps track of everybody you do business with so you can manage and service those relationships.

Applied correctly, CRM is the answer to the old question of how to stop wasting half your sales and marketing money. But you can't apply it correctly in a vacuum. Next, we'll talk about some of the ways to incorporate it into your general sales system.

Marketing Automation

Marketing automation is a subset of your CRM tools. Though it's not a system in its own right, it's important enough to call out specifically.

✓ At its core, marketing automation is any set of software systems that qualify and nurture leads without human interference.

✓ At its best, marketing automation lets you provide prospects with highly personalized content of direct interest that converts prospects into customers and customers into excited brand advocates.

✓ At present, "marketing automation" is a buzzword that people chase, looking for a hands-free, effortless engine to make them money. Used that way, even the best marketing-automation system falls short.

Done right, marketing automation turns your website into the most valuable member of your sales team. It works all day, every day; never asks for holidays or weekends off; doesn't charge overtime; and never tells an off-color joke in front of the HR manager.

Beyond that, strong marketing automation provides bankable benefits for your company by both *reducing the cost per sale* and *increasing the income from each of those cheaper sales.* That's a high-octane, double-whammy perfect storm of profit.

But Don't Get Cocky

Those benefits only come to companies that *do it right,* and there are a *lot* of ways to do it wrong. Research shows that people who buy marketing automation suites rarely use them fully. They become overwhelmed with the system's complexity and only scratch the surface of what a robust, properly leveraged marketing-automation system can do. That means the investment of capital and time pays off slowly, if at all.

To get the most out of your marketing-automation system, avoid these rookie mistakes:

✓ *Fire and forget.* Although it will complete tasks automatically, you will still need to test, monitor, assess, and update your system. The perfect lead-nurturing formula is a moving target, so you must adjust your aim from time to time.

✓ *Narrow scope.* A surprising number of businesses that adopt marketing automation use it only for email. The best systems also incorporate social media, landing pages, time tracking, and program management.

✓ *Getting spammy with it.* This is the most common problem in marketing automation and why almost 80 percent of people ignore marketing emails they've subscribed to. High value is key, even if it means sending emails with lower frequency.

✓ *Skimping on setup.* Major studies in the academic and market-research sectors show that most businesses that buy marketing automation never set up its most powerful resources. Learn how to use everything you need, even if that means bringing in a consultant.

✓ *Overreliance.* Far too many companies lean too heavily on automated marketing and take resources away from lead generation and face-to-face sales. Marketing automation is a force multiplier, but a million times zero is still zero.

The Right Tool for the Right Job

Once your marketing automation is set up and working well, you can trust it to do two specific jobs better than anything else in your company: *qualifying leads* and *nurturing leads*.

Qualifying leads. If you're using inbound digital marketing the way we've been telling you, your sales team should be extremely busy. They need to focus on the most qualified and ready-to-buy prospects. You can set up your marketing-automation software to do this via a variety of metrics.

Nurturing leads. What happens with the leads who don't yet qualify for your sales team's attention? If you ignore them, some other sales team will be happy to give them a call. Instead, your marketing-automation system will use the same metrics it uses to ping your sales team. It will set up a series of communication alerts pegged to metrics and behaviors, sending content to leads to keep you front-of-mind as a knowledgeable adviser.

The key here is to understand what marketing automation is good for and to use it without fail in those areas without trying to shoehorn it into other roles.

Project Management

Last comes project management, where the work of the company actually gets done.

You are familiar with project management, or you wouldn't be in the position you're in. You probably took a class in it at college or in your first job as a manager. You might be certified in one of the branded project-management systems, like PMP and Six Sigma.

There are many kinds of project management, from Scrum to waterfall; regardless of what methodology you subscribe to, project management plays an essential role in getting things done while on the job, in your home, or on vacation. If done correctly, project management can help you project costs, ensure a quality product, and build a stronger company.

The twenty-first century hasn't changed project management that much. It's still the same set of basic tasks:

✓ Breaking down timelines into deadlines

✓ Attaching milestones to timelines

✓ Assigning tasks to milestones

✓ Assigning people and teams to tasks

✓ Tracking time

✓ Providing accountability

The difference is that it can now be automated to help your company run more smoothly and reduce quality-control issues.

New project management features:

✓ Client task assignment and review

✓ Automatic milestone shifting

✓ Task and/or project templates

✓ Time reporting

✓ Project financial breakdowns

A few of the tools I see and recommend most with clients are Wrike, Scrum/Kanban, Zoho Projects, and Mavenlink.

CHAPTER 16
CHOOSING YOUR KNOWLEDGEMENT SYSTEMS

"And now is the time for me to talk with you about knowledgement," I said.

"Knowledgement?" said Chuck. "Stop making up words."

"It's a portmanteau word," I said.

"What did I just tell you about making up words?"

"I'm not! A portmanteau word is one that combines two words into a single word. Like jackalope," I said.

"Or masshole?" said Carole.

"And what two words are you combining in knowledgement?"

"Knowledge and management," Carole said.

"Yes, indeedy," I said.

"And why are we talking about knowledgement?" asked Chuck.

"You need some," I said.

"Why do you think that?" asked Carole.

"Because I've never worked with a company that didn't need more than they already had. Even companies that really have it all together. Even companies that do knowledgement services as their core product."

"Okay," said Chuck, "tell me more ..."

I mentioned in the last chapter how important it is to use systems to track your knowledge base. The bad news is just how much knowledge even smaller companies need to track and how poorly you are almost certainly tracking that knowledge right now.

The good news is, you don't have to reinvent the wheel. There's a *ton* of solid, functional knowledge-management software suites out there. It's just a matter of choosing the right one.

But first, let's look at the most common knowledgement system of all.

"Ask Bob"

Almost every company in the world has a Bob. He's been working there forever but never quite made it above the rank of team lead. Sometimes he has an attitude about that because he's had seniority over his last three bosses. But he's not going anywhere until he retires.

The thing about Bob is, he *knows everything*. Those new bosses come to him with questions about everything from how to put in a request for vacation to where the stapler is likely to be. Despite his low rank, higher-ups keep coming to him with basic questions. Almost every new hire orientation includes the trainer saying, "If you're not sure, ask Bob."

Asking Bob is efficient in some ways and popular because it's the path of least resistance. It has the added benefit that Bob likes it. It helps him feel more important and less frustrated with his lack of upward mobility in the company. Everybody wins.

Unless Bob is out sick or on vacation when somebody needs to ask him something.

Until Bob retires.

Unless Bob gets fed up and stops answering questions.

And that's why asking Bob is a problem. It introduces a single point of failure to the basic function of your company. Without Bob, things grind to a halt.

So, with no offense intended to the Bobs of the world, you absolutely must replace him with knowledgement software.

What Does Knowledgement Software Do?

Simply put, knowledgement software is your virtual Bob. It's software where things get put that people in your company need to know, which includes easy and intuitive ways to get the information back out when needed.

IBM developed a basic model for knowledgement systems that divided the tasks of knowledgement software into four buckets:

✓ Harvesting and codifying information about the company, its procedures, and its resources

✓ Harnessing the power of people with a directory of contact information, positions, and expertise

✓ Hunting for information through easy access, indexing, and search capacities

✓ Accommodating the possibility of growth with cultural support, chat rooms, groupware, and other ways to facilitate teamwork and collaboration

Whether it's Bob, or a bunch of folders, or a wiki, your business has some kind of knowledgement system in place for all of those tasks. Knowledgement software puts it where everybody can use it, so the people in your company can focus on their core tasks while still having the support of your institutional memory.

What Features Do You Need?

The top feature you will need for your knowledgement software is an API and the ability to integrate with other systems. That is because no one knowledgement suite will handle everything you need,[26] and you *will* need to integrate a couple of systems to create something comprehensive.

---

26   More on that in a bit.

Other features to look for in any knowledgement software include:

KNOWLEDGE MANAGEMENT PLATFORM	CUSTOMER RELATIONSHIP MANAGEMENT	PROJECT MANAGEMENT
• Information management • Team collaboration • Accessible and searchable reporting • Easy to use • Revision history • API	• Contact management • Reporting and dashboards • Lead management • Deals and tasks • Campaign management • Email tracking • Social media management • API	• Project planning and scheduling • Team collaboration • Time-tracking reporting • Project budgeting • Billing and quotes • API

You will also want to focus on a few key features for the kinds of knowledgement you need most. If your CRM is strong but your project management is weak, you'll need different features than a company with good project management and poor knowledge resources.

There Is No One Solution

At Nuanced Media, we value strong knowledgement so much that we make it part of our core services. I've looked at hundreds of knowledgement suites for dozens of industry niches, and I can say only one thing is universally true of every single one of them:

There is no system that does everything you need it to do.
Some are great at managing lead information but bad at handling policies and procedures. Others track financials and benchmarks well but lack a directory.

The truth is, you'll need to install two or three knowledgement suites and then develop a bespoke system for integrating them all. Often that system can simply be an intranet site, but you still will need to put something in place.

I never promised you good news all the time. I only promised you the truth.

PART 2
LEADS AND THE ART OF THE CLOSE
EXECUTIVE SUMMARY

In this section, we'll discuss:

- How closing has changed and stayed the same since the internet changed everything

- The nature of a the twenty-first century engineered sales pipeline

- Nonqualifying leads and what to do with them

- The power of analytics in modern closing

CHAPTER 17
MULTIPLE CLOSEGASMS

"You ready to talk about sales?" I said to Chuck.

"Only if you'll tell me something I don't know."

"That's a challenge for somebody with your experience, but I'm up for it."

"Try me."

"Who's the most important member of your sales team?"

"That would by Marie Han. She could sell tennis shoes to a donkey with no legs."

"Wrong."

"Okay. I'll bite."

"Your website."

"I've seen the numbers, Ryan. Marie wins by a landslide. We're talking Reagan second-term landslide here. Hands down."

"That's because you're not using your website correctly. Used right, your website will manage leads automatically, twenty-four hours a day, without charging you commissions. It will respond immediately to consumer inquiries and sort leads by quality. All for free."

"So you want me to replace Marie?"

"No. I want you to set up your website so it makes Marie even better and more efficient at her job. Your income rises. She gets more commissions. Everybody wins. Here's how."

The classic noir movie *The Way of the Gun* includes the line, "The greatest distance between two points is a kidnapper and his money." They were close to right, but really the prize goes to the distance between a lead and a customer.

One of the few drawbacks of the inbound marketing method is how far along that distance somebody is when they first make contact with your company. In the old days, 57 percent of people who contacted a company already had made up their minds that they were inclined to both buy from and do business with that vendor. A higher percentage of closes came out of each contact, though the model left less opportunity to influence somebody who hadn't yet made a decision to buy.

Modern profit engineering makes first contact with a potential buyer far sooner. This earlier acquisition is as much of a game-changer for the lead-nurturing and closing process as the internet was to the attraction stage.

How It Was

The traditional model of working a lead to a sale ran through three steps:

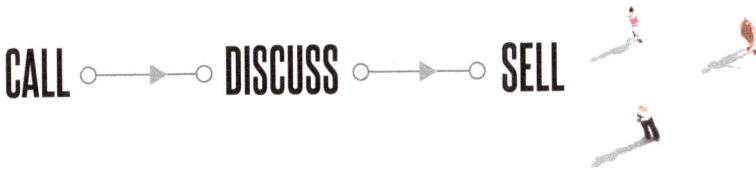

CALL ○——▶—○ **DISCUSS** ○——▶—○ **SELL**

An interested lead would call in directly to the sales department or fill out a form requesting a call. The salesperson built rapport, answered questions, offered discounts, presold, made promises,[27] tested closes, and generally spent time nurturing a lead. The discussion might take one call or might take several conversations, including some on-the-house drinks and/or dinners, depending on the potential value of the sale.

The final stage of this older model was the sale itself. That stage didn't change substantially from era to era, with one huge exception. In

---

27 Which may or may not have been kept.

the old way, the sale was the end of the process. Modern sales require nurturing existing clients just as you would leads.

We'll talk about that part in another chapter, but here we need to look at how the process has changed from beginning to end.

How It Is

If you're selling cars or life insurance, the old adage "Always be closing" is exactly what it sounds like. Every sentence out of your mouth, every action, should move leads one step closer to signing on the dotted line.

That's because those models bring potential buyers to the door much closer to the buying stage than does profit engineering. Similarly, those B2C customers are dealing with lower stakes and lower budgets than the B2B decision-makers you deal with.

For those reasons, the process here is an iterative series of contacts. Each of those contacts also moves toward a "close," but until the very end, that close isn't a full purchase. Here's how it works:

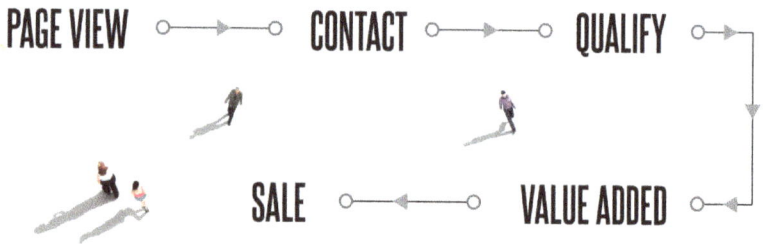

Let's look at each of those in turn: what they are, why they exist, and how they work.

Page View

This is the most important part of understanding how to manage leads in a modern, inbound profit engineering system. Inbound leads have a 1–10 percent close rate, on average, depending on the industry and how a company handles their sales cycle. This is *not* because inbound leads are less effective. It's because inbound sales hook potential buyers earlier in the game.

Why hook people so much earlier in a process, at a time when they might not even be close to ready to buy? Because research shows that 35 to 50 percent of sales go to the vendors that customers contact first. Put another way, no matter how far from buying somebody might be when they access your online content, when they do buy, they'll buy from you ... if your online content is memorable and powerful enough for readers to remember you when they're ready to buy. This means the first job of your online content is to hook and groom readers for later interactions with your sales team.

Contact

Because of what we just talked about, having your sales team contact everybody who viewed your page would waste company resources and frustrate your salespeople. Before that first contact happens, you must leverage one of the hidden superpowers of well-executed digital marketing. Remember a few chapters ago when I described your company website as the best salesperson in your company? This stage is why.

A well-designed, well-executed inbound marketing system guides buyers from casual interest to ready to buy before your human salespeople ever make contact.

It does that automatically, twenty-four hours a day, while costing you nothing for all the extra hours. It's not free to set up, but once the system's in place, the actual cost per qualified, interested lead is negligible.

That well-designed, well-executed system performs this impressive task by doing the following things:

✓ Capturing the attention of casually interested readers via high-value content

✓ Guiding readers to further information automatically with calls to action and internal links

✓ Identifying where readers are along their buyer's journey

✓ Assessing whether or not a lead is qualified

✓ Leading qualified buyers to an offer that delivers value and triggers contact from your human sales team

Such a system lets your salespeople work smart instead of hard. If they had to contact everybody who visited your site, the close rate would embarrass them. More important, they wouldn't have time to give your qualified leads the attention they need and deserve. By letting your automated inbound marketing system sort visitors, you set up your sales team to call only the leads most likely to result in a sale.

Qualifying

The other hazard of hooking people earlier in the buying process is that fewer of them are confirmed qualified buyers. This is the first stage in which that "closing toward something that's not quite a close" really starts to both become clear and show its power.

At Nuanced Media, after a potential client has seen enough of our content to want to sit with us and find out what we can do for them, we set a meeting and show—in detail—how, what, and why we do what we do. We won't work with a client unless we can project at least a three-times return on investment for them.

As that meeting draws to a close, we offer to build a market-velocity action plan (MVAP) with the potential client. During this process, we sit down with the key decision-makers from the now "partners" team during a series of meetings and discover the top opportunities for their company, based on industry research, standardized sales-pipeline metrics, historical data, and their highest margin product or service line. After discovering their top financial and operational opportunities, we lay out a strategy to execute on these opportunities and project low, medium, and high financial returns. If the medium projection exceeds a three-times ROI, then we will recommend that we work with the partner to execute the MVAP.[28]

This process works for a number of reasons.

First, it gives massive value to our potential client. Our MVAP

---

28 You can download an example of an MVAP at @@.

includes expert strategy, industry benchmarks, financial projections, and a list of top-growth opportunities. Any client could take the MVAP and use it to engineer their profit destiny without our help … but they won't because it demonstrates how well we do the job they are considering hiring us to do.

Second, it lays out for our client the costs, initiatives, risks, and rewards of working with us. It allows an educated decision with reduced risk.

Third, it helps us make a final qualification check on the client. If they are unable to afford the MVAP or unwilling to follow through on our recommendations, or if our two companies are simply a poor cultural fit for one another, we can know early on that this partnership won't work well enough to delight the client. It lets everybody pull out before things start to go wrong.

After years of giving away something slightly less labor-intensive for free, we found this works better.

It works better because anybody who can't afford our $2,500 introduction absolutely cannot afford our core product. It's better to know that early in the process, so you waste neither the lead's time nor your own efforts.

This doesn't mean you just drop an unqualified lead. It's rude, and they can still help your business grow. But because the later steps in this dance cost you time and money, it's best to make sure you take them only with qualified partners.

The Value-Added Loop

In the bad old days, discussion was limited to face-to-face meetings, where the sales rep spent the whole time looking for a solid close.

In a well-engineered system, discussion happens in two parts:

1. The part you're already familiar with: the discussion between a live sales representative and the lead. This requires no real explanation to the kind of business leader who reads this book, but do understand that it happens second chronologically.

2. The part that happens automatically, via an email lead-nurturing system. We discussed this in detail in earlier chapters.

The details of these points are what we'll spend the rest of this part of the book discussing. Right now, the important thing to keep in mind is that you're in for *more than one discussion.*

Again, because leads start the journey much farther from ready-to-buy than in earlier modes, it's best to look at discussion as a loop. Each content with a lead adds value to the relationship and looks to move one step closer to a solid sale … but can also lead to *another* discussion of either type.

That's why we call this the "discussion loop." You'll move through several iterations of the loop with each lead. Some might go through it just once, while others will go through it several times—each of which is unique and adds value—until finally being ready to buy.

And how do you keep track of each lead as they move through these iterative discussions? I'm glad you asked.

CHAPTER 18
THE SALES PIPELINE

"Tell me about your sales pipeline," I said to Chuck.

"We'll have to bring Marie in on that one," he said. *"I don't watch the details on that."*

"That's closer to the right answer than you might think," I responded.

"What do you mean? I figured you'd tell me I should have all of that information ready to hand at all times."

"Ready to hand doesn't mean in your head," I told him. *"Especially with an automated pipeline. With those, you have all the information you need ready when you need it, but you don't have to spend time or sales resources unless it needs direct human intervention."*

"I like the sound of that. Tell me more."

As a successful business person, you already understand the basic definition of a sales pipeline. As a business person in the twenty-first century, it's likely you don't completely have a handle on what's possible with a profit-engineered, digital-sales pipeline with all the trimmings.

Sales Pipeline:

1. Attraction
2. Conversion
3. Close
    a. Lead
    b. Qualified lead
    c. Consultative sales
    d. Sale
    e. Set up triggers for additional sales opportunities
4. Advocacy

Let's take a peek at the best practices and worst rookie mistakes of engineering your twenty-first–century profit pipeline.

Best Practices

I'm an expert because I watch people succeed, day in and day out, and I pay attention to the patterns that emerge. Although each business's pipeline will be unique, the most successful pipelines share a handful of common traits:

They focus on flow. An excellent sales pipeline has both the motivation and the means to move from one stage to the next, baked into all of its content. It's considered carefully in design and executed well in practice.

They qualify leads. By searching for the no, you can get a lot done, save time, and be more efficient. Are you the decision-maker? Typically, the investment for this starts around a gajillion dollars. How do you feel about those numbers? What is your procurement process? Is this a value or cost decision?

They provide accurate and timely responses to questions and inquiries. Most of the time, this is in the form of an email or other automated prompt. Sometimes it's an alert sent to a live human sales or customer-service rep.

They track individual leads accurately and automatically. This is simple and exactly what it sounds like. I'm consistently surprised how often it doesn't happen.

They provide value-added content that speaks to the most common pain points for the customer profiles. These build your credibility and leverage your authority while simultaneously making the lead progressively more invested in a relationship with your brand.

They emphasize consultative sales, especially for the highest-ticket items. This helps alleviate the sense of risk to a buyer's job or reputation by putting your team in the role of adviser and coach, as opposed to high-pressure sales.

Over time they refine their target market. By tracking the actions and characteristics of various leads, they can help you develop a system for assigning different content and pipes for different types of clients. This means less wasted time, higher sales ratios, and more profit.

These factors combine to make your sales pipeline a tool for measuring and improving your sales metrics. It provides topical, timely, and accurate motion in casual leads until those leads become ready for contact with a live member of your team.

How Not to Screw Yours Up

Some aspects of the Perfect Digital Sales Pipeline™ are still being developed, but a lot of smart people have made a lot of money using what we've figured out so far. Here, then, are the top ten rookie mistakes I've made and seen made. Avoid them at all costs.

Incorrect setup. Many excellent systems aren't leveraged to their full potential because nobody sets them up correctly. Bake time into your onboarding schedule to fully understand the system's pieces, parts, and potential. Set them up for optimal use by your team.

Overautomation. It can be tempting to automate everything possible in your sales pipeline, but many mistakes are tempting. The personal touch remains important (especially in high-priced B2B products).

Treating all leads equally. I've mentioned before and will mention again that qualified and unqualified leads must be triaged and handled differently from one another. Make this process part of the design of your pipeline from step one.

Failing to incorporate CRM. Customer-relationship management tools are a huge boon to your sales system, but I see too many companies treating them as separate from the sales funnel. Every company (from a solopreneur keeping everything in this "wetware" to a multinational using $100,000/month software) has to manage customers, knowledge, and projects. The more that systems for that management are linked and talk with one another, the better your profit management will function.

Firing and forgetting. Automated systems need watching, analyzing, tweaking, and adjustment. Always watch your numbers and compare them to goals and industry averages. Consistently make changes to the weakest points until your sales pipeline engine is tuned up to the max.

Spending too much time managing. The numbers that modern metrics produce are attractive and infinite in their complexity. It can be easy to "rabbit hole" into things that don't help much. Avoid diminishing returns by focusing on that 20 percent that brings you 80 percent of your returns.

Failing to differentiate customers. Know your target markets and know the difference between your types of customers. Don't treat client profile A the same way you would client profile B. Their personalities are different. And don't invest as much money and time on a $5,000 customer as you would on a $100,000 lead.

Not having upsell opportunities. You already know that it's easier and more profitable to sell to existing clients than to close new leads. Apply it here by adding upsell opportunities to your pipeline, client management, and other things that focus on lifetime value for clients.

The good news here is that you already have a reasonable sense of what makes a sales pipeline work. The bad news is that a lot of the details have changed since you graduated from B-school.

The better news is, once you understand the changes, you'll be able to apply them again and again to vastly increase your profits.

CHAPTER 19

THE POWER OF ANALYTICS

"So we have a plan. Or you're going to give us a plan. How long until we're all done?" Chuck asked.

"Oh, you're never done. "

"What do you mean we're never done?"

"Nobody gets it right on the first try. Not even you and me working together. And even when you get something right, things can change so it stops being right. "

"Are you going to hit me up for an extended service plan?"

"No. We don't do that. Those things are piracy."

"Okay. Then what are you going to do?"

"I'm going to talk about analytics."

Nobody ever got into the Olympics by just practicing a sport without being told how they were doing. A few people got to the open tryouts that way, and they got their butts swiftly handed to them by people who'd had the benefit of proper coaching. A good coach doesn't just tell athletes how to perform; they watch athletes and tell them how to improve. They provide feedback based on current performance so athletes can do better the next time. Without that feedback, athletes are flying blind.

It's just the same with your sales metrics. Without some way of measuring your performance, you can't improve systematically or even accurately. You have no way of establishing a baseline or building a plan of action. Like that uncoached athlete, you are flying blind.

You need analytics. Remember in the last section when I mentioned CRM and marketing automation? Here's where those really start to shine. Let's look at both kinds of analytics systems and how they can help you get more traction in your business-growth journey.

Marketing-Automation Analytics

As you'll remember from earlier, marketing-automation software contacts leads without human interference, sending them content and calls to action at various points in their travel from "just looking" to "ready to buy."

Marketing-automation software also reports to you what's going on with each lead you onboard into the system. These reports are the raw performance data that lets you coach yourself to improve the performance of your entire sales pipeline. The most important metrics it reports on include:

Conversion Rate
Each business development plan you load into your automation must be set up in stages as the buyer becomes more seriously interested in your product. Each stage must send different kinds of content, messaging, and calls to action. The rates and timing of customer progress from

one stage to the next[29] can indicate which parts of your business-development content are working ... and which aren't even being opened.

Lead-Nurturing Rates
Email open rates, social media activation, click-through rates, and similar indicators show you how often leads interact meaningfully with the content you send them. Analytics of these factors tell you how engaged leads are with your brand, what email subjects catch their eye, which reports and emails get the most traction, and where your leads are losing interest.

Occurrence of Triggered Events
How often do leads visit your pricing page, load something into the shopping cart without buying, read how to request a demo, or perform other activities on your site that show an escalation in their level of interest? This analytic helps you fine-tune your sales system while simultaneously showing which pieces of content most reliably and frequently trigger that shift.

Web Page Visits
Every page of your website is a full-time sales team member operating day and night, every day of the year, for free—or it would be if the copy on the page and the links to the page operated optimally. Good marketing-automation analytics let you know, page by page, how your site performs. It will tell you which pages you should imitate and which ones you should rework.

Customer-Relationship Management
What marketing automation is for your website and content emails, CRM software is for your sales department. These suites track a lead's progress through both automated sales systems and human team members to improve your sales and customer experiences.

---

29   Including the actual purchase.

Just as with marketing-automation software, good CRM software provides analytics for your sales systems. However, the specific metrics it reports are different.

Progress through the Stages of the Sales Pipeline

A full sale progresses through every stage in your sales pipeline. Lost leads stop at some point in the process, and CRM analytics tell you exactly where. You can identify logjams and "broken" stages and determine which routes in a differentiated pipeline are getting the most and fewest completed sales.

Win/Loss Ratios

Each stage and action in your sales system either loses a lead or wins by bringing them to the next stage of the process. A breakdown of exactly how many wins and losses a team member, script, email, or action generates provides vital intelligence for tweaking your system, rewriting your content, and coaching your sales team.

Sales Revenue Sourcing

You would be amazed at the number of businesses I work with that begin our relationship knowing how much *total* sales they get in a given period but have no idea how much comes from their sales team versus automated web sales versus walk-in traffic. You simply cannot put your sales and marketing resources where they need to be without that information.

Cost of Acquisition

Do you know how much it costs to acquire a viable lead and onboard them into your marketing system? Or how much it costs to get that lead from there to the beginning of your sales pipeline? How much to get from that point to your first sale? And the average value of that sale? The data is the answer to that old saw about knowing you waste half your marketing dollars without knowing which half.

The Bottom Line

All the information I just gave you does you no good if you don't put it to work. By applying the analytics from both your marketing-automation suite and your CRM software, you will be able to direct and correct your sales pipeline across a wide array of factors. These include (but are far from limited to):

✓ Iterative improvements to each part of your system for more leads and sales gained more efficiently

✓ Creating more accurate sales forecasts to better manage cash flow

✓ Focusing on the 20% of the leads and customers who are responsible for 80% of your sales to turbocharge your profits

✓ Setting your company up for explosive growth

PART 1
ESTABLISHING BRAND ADVOCACY
EXECUTIVE SUMMARY

In this section, we'll discuss:

- Building a community around your brand
- The dos and don'ts of social media community
- Leveraging unqualified leads

CHAPTER 20
BUILDING A COMMUNITY AROUND YOUR BRAND

"Chuck," I asked, "what kind of music do you like?"

"Big band–era marches and smooth jazz. Why?"

"Okay. That won't work. How about you, Carole?"

"Mostly eighties heavy metal, with a little bit of hip- hop when I don't think anybody's watching."

"That works."

"What works?" asked Chuck.

"When was the last time you went a week without seeing an AC/DC T-shirt?"

"What?" said Chuck.

"How would you like people to proudly wear your brand on a T-shirt and collect multiple shirts showing off different times they interacted with your brand?"

"Just like with rock concerts," said Carole.

"It doesn't quite work with big band–era marches," I admitted. "They just don't have the traction."

"What do you mean?" said Chuck. "John Phillip Sousa is the man! He composed more than one hundred thirty marches in his life. He has a musical instrument named after him!"

"Thank you for making his point," said Carole.

I've spent a lot of time showing you how modern, digital, inbound profit engineering can bring more qualified leads to your virtual door and help you sell larger contracts to more of them. It's all about providing remarkable content to everybody. That includes visitors, leads, and (maybe/someday) people alike.

You could just stop there and increase your revenues significantly, but that would be a huge mistake. Just because somebody puts money on the table doesn't mean it's time to abandon that customer. We are not used-car salesmen wearing jackets almost as checkered as our pasts. We are modern, digital business developers, and we know the value of a customer only begins at the close of the first sale.

By the same token, we are not boiler-room appointment setters who hang up on nonqualified leads and scratch them out of our books. We are—say it with me now—modern, digital profit engineers. We know people who can't buy our product directly still have massive potential value for our brands. Building community is how we develop and leverage the value of both past clients and qualified customers, so let's talk about how. But first, let's address the biggest question in this conversation:

Why Bother?

Building community takes consistent application of a lot of effort. Because it means responding to things in real time, it even requires staff you have to pay for. It's a lot more resource-intensive than the automated sales-pipeline web tools we've discussed so far. So why do it?

Building community keeps you in touch with people who aren't actively buying from you but still feel positive about your brand. By keeping in touch, you lead them to still feel more positively toward your brand as the community grows.

Musicians have demonstrated the power of this for decades by not just selling albums but also creating communities of devoted fans. That fan base includes people who have purchased every album, T-shirt, boxed set, and concert ticket, as well as people who couldn't afford to buy albums at all. But go mention Iron Maiden in a room full of heavy metal fans or Loreena McKennitt to a group of New Age listeners, and watch the community go to work.

> **"** *Since we're talking about music, here's something to know about value-added content.*
>
> *In the late 1990s, the internet started making it really easy to pirate music. The Recording Industry Association of America (and Metallica, those short-haired bastards) kicked up a huge fuss about it. (See also book publishing and movie pirating.)*
>
> *But here's the thing: everybody who looks at the numbers knows that the piracy hasn't significantly eroded profits. That's because everybody who steals an album (or whatever) becomes a member of the fan community, one of those unqualified leads that are so valuable to profit engineering.*
>
> *It speaks to the value of giving things away for free to engage people around your brand. Even when an entire industry fights to not give it away, it builds a base of engaged fans. Think about the power of giving it away on purpose.*

What music publicists understand and digital marketers must embrace is the value and power of those community members. Members of a brand community frequently:

- ✓ Share information about the brand with qualified buyers they know.

- ✓ Write favorable online reviews.

- ✓ Engage passionately against negative reviews, refuting spurious claims and voicing alternative opinions.

- ✓ Write articles or blog posts about the brand or its products.

- ✓ Act as evangelists for the brand.

- ✓ Add robust content to the community social media pages to give it more momentum and gravitas.

Polls from the last two years found that 55 percent of consumers are willing to recommend companies that delight them. They further found that friends who received such recommendations will buy, even if it means paying a higher price than with a competitor.

The Elements of Strong Community

Think about Kia cars. There's nothing wrong with them, but nobody's getting passionate about the brand. Now think about the Ford versus Chevy debate that's been part of US car culture since those brands began.

That's powerful brand loyalty.

But wait! There's more.

Now think about how people feel about their Harley-Davidson motorcycles. Think about how some people who don't even own Harleys think about Harleys.

You don't just want a community, like the group of people who all drive Kias. You want a strong community like Ford and Chevy enthusiasts. If you can manage to develop a fanatical[30] community like Harley riders or Iron Maiden fans, more power to you—though, in truth, that level of community is as much a matter of luck as good planning with solid execution.

If you look at one hundred different successful brand communities, you get what looks like one hundred different strategies for building them. This makes sense on the surface because obviously the things that motivate and engage Chevy-driving men, bikers[31] on their hogs, or Maiden fans who "up the irons" are all different.

But look closer, and you will see that powerful communities share several traits in common.

They Exist to Serve the Community Itself
At the top level, a brand community is built to make a profit. However, every *decision* about the community should be made to benefit and serve

---

30 Remember—that's where the word "fan" comes from.
31 Or coders. Or lawyers.

a culture of fandom and the needs of the members. Build an authentic community based on what members ask for and the community will help build your brand. Ask people to buy into an inauthentic fan club, and your community will be stillborn.

They Look Spontaneous but Are Carefully Engineered
The daily interactions with fellow members and your company must be unscripted, but the development is a matter of careful cultivation. Strong, consistent messaging via communication hubs, thought leaders, community advocates, and the fan base are all carefully planned, with excellent execution of that plan.

They Embrace Constructive Conflict
A community for Coke never wants an argument about Coke versus Pepsi, but they thrive on arguments about Diet Coke versus Coke Zero or what spice mix to include in a Coke-based barbecue sauce. Internal factions and friendly conflicts make communities more interesting and members more engaged.

They Give Everybody a Role
They key factor in a community is membership, a sense of belonging. People can't belong if they lack a role to fit into. Not everyone is cut out to be a fan club president, online thought leader, or welcomer of the noobs. That said, everyone who wants a place should get a place where they can contribute and feel they belong.

They Gamify Participation
From free T-shirts for coming to a promotional event to online badges or even titles based on activity levels, strong communities use the human impulse to accumulate points and trophies as an engine to drive participation. The points needn't have value outside the community, but giving members some sort of objective can help ramp up activity.

I'm not saying that you have to be Coca-Cola or Harley Davidson to run a successful brand community. I am saying that you should look at brands that are successful with community building.

Analyze what they do, and work to replicate their success. Examine how they use their social media channels, online communities, and direct email campaigns to establish belonging and ownership among their clients and potential customers.

CHAPTER 21
THE DOS AND DON'TS OF SOCIAL MEDIA

"All righty, then. Social media." I said.

"I hate social media," Chuck said.

"Why?"

"I don't understand it. It's so easy to sink thousands of dollars into things that don't work, only to find some twenty-two-year-old's cat video went bacterial after he spent five bucks. "

"You don't understand how it works, but you understand that it works."

"I understand it can work, but I'm suspicious that most of its working is luck."

"And what does Lombardi say about luck?"

"Luck is where opportunity and preparation meet."

"That's the one."

"So you're saying you can show me how to prepare on social media so things work out when the opportunity appears?"

"Exactly."

"Okay. I'm listening."

Social media is either the best thing or the worst thing to happen to small businesses in the last hundred years.

✓ It's the *best* thing because it has fully democratized publicity. Even a home-based microbusiness can potentially reach billions with the right viral content and can foster a dedicated community of fans and advocates.

✓ It's the *worst* thing because doing it wrong, or not doing it at all, gives all your competitors who do it right a significant advantage over you.

There's a lot of art and science to doing it right, enough that entire books and e-courses have been written on the topic. For now, let's look at the top-level strategic dos and don'ts of building a social media community.

Do name your community.
The difference between "I'm a person who enjoys Monty Python" and "I'm a member of the International Ministry of Silly Walks (Parrot Division)" is immense. A named community gives a sense of belonging and begins the journey toward advocacy and rabid fandom. It's also easier to show on a business card or web post.

Don't skimp on organization and goals.
There's a persistent myth about social media that you *can't* or *shouldn't* subject it to standard business goal-setting, organization, benchmarks, and measurements. This is a myth. Your social media community strategy should be as formal and powerful as your strategy for any other branding effort.

Do ask (lots of) questions.
Questions foster discussion. Discussion creates engagement. Engagement builds community. When you post, end as many posts as possible with a question for your social media community members to answer.

When you respond to posts within the community, respond in a way that invites answers. This is a lot like the old cocktail party rule of asking two questions for each statement you make, and it works for exactly the same reasons.

Don't fire and forget.
Never post anything you're not prepared to follow up on. Posting something and then ignoring community responses is worse than never posting anything at all. The point of all this is to foster connection and build a community. That won't happen if there's no difference between your social media and a television ad.

Do act as a matchmaker.
Not romantically—unless that's your business model. At the top level, the existence of your community acts as an interest-based matchmaker by connecting people who are passionate about you and what you do. Within that broad scope, also find ways to help connect people over other commonalities. The easiest one is shared location so community members can meet up in real life. Other commonalities will appear as you watch the posts and communications and think about what makes your brand valuable and unique.

Don't be too professional.
On social media, you can easily be too professional by lacking transparency, responsiveness, humor, and a personal voice. One easy example is using "I" instead of "we" in social media communication. "we" recognizes that the exchange is between two human beings. With this being said, you should follow best social media practices by maintaining appropriate communications and not blowing your top when challenged.

Do focus on relationships.
This seems obvious, but based on many social media feeds I've seen, it isn't obvious enough. Your social community is about your relationship with your fans, their relationship with the brand, and their relationship

with each other. Every strategy and tactic should serve as many of those relationships as possible. There are no exceptions to this rule.

Don't automate.
Well, almost never automate. It's okay to batch-complete your social media shares and schedule them according to your content calendar. But always create an alert to have somebody watch those shares when they go out, and never, ever, *ever* automate your responses to engagement around what you post.

Do optimize your accounts.
Apply the most recent content-optimization strategies to your accounts, profiles, and shared content. What you do for your other online content, you should also do for your social media.

Don't be afraid to pay.
Watch your spending carefully—many social media pay-to-play programs are scams—but the right ones can boost viewership and membership by thousands of members over the course of a year. "Social media should be 100 percent free" is another myth you need to disbelieve for successful social media strategy.

Do prospect influencers and thought leaders.
I'm not telling you to stalk the people who are most influential in your industry and community … but you should definitely stalk the people who are most influential in your industry and community. Watch their feeds. Share their blogs. Comment insightfully within their communities. At worst, this leads to interesting conversations with people you respect. At best, it can create a mutually profitable partnership … and bring some of their fans over into your community.

Don't miss trending topics.
This strategy is so common it has a slang term *newsjacking*. Whether you're an online content company (ahem) posting about how many tweets the Super Bowl or presidential election got or a legal firm posting

on a recent scandal, it pays to write about what other people are reading. This isn't cheating. It's solid strategy.

Do track and measure.
Social media is absolutely measurable and trackable if you know what the various metrics mean. Don't fall for the myth that it isn't. Set goals, create metrics to track your progress toward those goals, review both regularly, and recalibrate to match.

As I said earlier, the detailed how-to and resources for each of these are beyond the scope of this book and are the job of the expert minions with whom you have surrounded yourself. Just keep these navigation points in mind while building your social media community strategy, and hold your people accountable to these guiding lights.

How to Build a Community
The great thing is that if you already have an existing business with customers, then you are halfway there. Quite frequently we find the largest ROI on a marketing campaign is targeting existing customers and letting them know of the additional services your company provides.

Most people do this but do it poorly. They contact existing or previous clients, only to sell them things (which is always off-putting; you have that one friend like that, and you resent him). Or they do it in a random way, unconnected to the overall strategy. Or they only do it once in a while, when somebody thinks to do it.

Here are some of the best ways I've found to systematically build a community and keep it vibrant:

- ✓ **Include all leads in your community emails**. Not everyone is market-qualified, but everyone can be a member of your community.

- ✓ **Leverage the content you create**, using all of your thought leadership content to bring people into your sales funnel.

- ✓ **Never sell**, but always add value and work to establish yourself as a trusted guide and expert.

✓ **Segment your community** so the right people get the right content. This keeps people from mentally dumping your updates into the spam bucket.

✓ **Reward participation** with recognition and tangible prizes for the people who are most actively engaged.

✓ **Use surveys and simple questions** to ask your community how you can do better.

✓ **Provide upsell opportunities** periodically. This is tough to balance against the directive to never be "salesy," but it can tap a gold mine of previously unrealized income.

✓ **Leverage old content from time to time** so new members can interact with your most successful and popular content.

Building community is like tending a garden. If neglected, the flowers and fruits and veggies can die. You'll have an empty plot of land that's useless except for sucking up some of your time and regret a few times each year. In the worst cases, the weeds you let grow can choke things out and kill the entire project.

But with careful feeding, watering, weeding, and planning, that garden can grow into the kind of crop that feeds your family[32] for a long time.

---

32   And the families of all your team members.

CHAPTER 22
LEVERAGING UNQUALIFIED LEADS

"Now is where we talk about what to do with all those unqualified leads,"
I said.

"That's easy," said Chuck. "Dump 'em. They're a waste of time and resources."

"Nope," I said.

"What?" said Chuck.

"Whatever are you talking about?" asked Carole.

"Have you ever been to a car lot and had a salesman snub you because you weren't interested in a high-ticket auto?"

"It's been a while, but yes."

"Or had a waiter or bartender give you bad service because they thought you weren't going to tip?"

"Yes," said Chuck and Carole together.

Carole went on, "This one time I got snark from a saleslady at a nice dress shop because I came in wearing jeans and a T-shirt."

"Okay," I said. "When you talk about those businesses later, what do you say about them?"

"Oh," said Chuck.

"Some of those unqualified buyers can be the best drivers of your community."

"Tell me more," said Chuck.

You've had the kinds of experiences I just talked about with Chuck and Carole. Remaining warm with your unqualified leads is good karma. It's also smart business.

Three Reasons Not to Ignore Unqualified Leads

Unqualified leads might not buy today, but that doesn't mean they can't help you grow your business. In my experience, I've found this is true for three reasons.

Not now doesn't mean not ever. Each lead had some reason for contacting you, even if it wasn't to make a purchase that day. If you establish yourself as a friendly and helpful expert now, you'll be the first vendor called when a lead becomes qualified.

This is a long-term game but pays off surprisingly well. A few of the unqualified leads who fit into this category include:

- ✓ Students preparing to enter the industry. They'll use your stuff for papers and later remember you when they're in a position to buy.

- ✓ Lower-level employees and gatekeepers. They might be tasked with research or report to people who do make decisions. Though you may never do business with them, they will influence the people you will do business with.

- ✓ Up-and-comers. These folks might not be buyers today, but you can bet they'll be buyers down the road. And they'll remember who was cool to them "back in the day."

You never know who people know. *This* particular lead might not be ready to buy but may influence somebody who is. If they feel slighted by you, they will mention that. If you treat them well, they'll mention that too.

Anybody who has tried to date somebody who was friends with somebody who didn't like them knows the pain of making this mistake. In B2B sales, this particularly applies to:

✓ Office managers, personal assistants, and minions. The ultimate buyer of your product will often send somebody to make first contact. They are often fiercely protective of these team members, and you blow one off at your peril.

✓ Friends and family. It's not fair and it's not right, but if a CEO's kid has a bad experience with you, you can kiss that CEO's business goodbye.

✓ Colleagues and rivals. At this stage in your career, you've participated in at least one industry conference or get-together where everybody dissed a particular vendor. Blowing off unqualified leads is a good way to become the dissed vendor in question.

Advocates aren't always customers. Many unqualified leads are simply interested in the space where you do business. They are hobbyists and professionals without buying power. These people talk—in real life and online—with other enthusiasts. If they feel valued and given value by you, they will spread the word.

Look at the list for "not now doesn't mean not ever" for the sort of folks who often fall into this category. Add to it retirees and hobbyists. Those two categories are some of the most passionate people in any industry and often become thought leaders themselves. They can generate millions in sales without ever making a purchase themselves.

So How to Track Them Effectively?

If the answer is "Don't blow off your unqualified leads because you might need them later," then that begs the question of how to track them without wasting time and money.

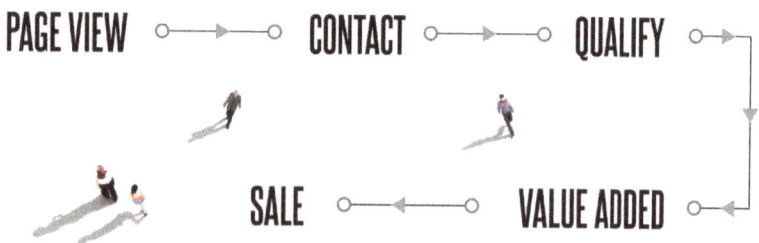

PAGE VIEW ○——▶——○ CONTACT ○——▶——○ QUALIFY ○——▶

SALE ○——◀——○ VALUE ADDED ○——◀—┘

That second answer is one of those things that's simple once you set it up but does take some focus and effort to get set up in the first place. Here's how you do it.

Qualified but Unwanted Leads

There's another category of leads and customers nobody likes to talk about but everybody knows is out there: people who might do business with you but who you don't want to do business with.

Toxic, unwanted leads and clients come in all shapes and sizes, but they often share a few key traits or behaviors:

- ✓ Ignoring your advice (especially if they gripe about the results afterward)

- ✓ Constant complaints about small issues or factors that are universal across the industry

- ✓ Micromanaging you into making decisions that aren't right for the product or brand

- ✓ Being unresponsive or indecisive

- ✓ Not respecting your staff, time, or expertise

- ✓ Consistently paying late or trying to renegotiate contracts

- ✓ Costing more in time and labor than their business justifies

You should run screaming from these leads, and gently fire them if they are already clients. At best, they will take time away from more profitable and less stress-inducing clients. At worst, their toxic attitude will poison parts of your own company culture.

Or you can go big and apply a trick one of our chief strategists first used while working for Home Depot.

He identified the bottom 10 percent of their B2B clients—the ones who always complained, returned stuff all the time, paid their accounts late, and generally caused more trouble than they were worth.

Then he contacted each of them and recommended they do business with Lowe's.

This is evil-genius–level maneuvering. Take those unwanted clients and leads, and give them to your competitors. Some of them will be a better match for that company culture, and the others will give you a meaningful, if slightly dastardly, advantage.

Before good automation and email, it was often too costly to nurture your relationship with these unqualified leads. It simply took too many resources to hand-manage everything and print the correspondence.

Today, though, things are very different. You can keep the unqualified leads on your books indefinitely and communicate with them essentially for free. As each brings you business of one sort of another, they become a source of free money.

And everybody likes free money.

PART 2
CUSTOMER-DRIVEN SUCCESS
EXECUTIVE SUMMARY

In this section, we'll discuss:

• How to impact clients to develop them into powerful brand advocates

• Using customer feedback as an essential part of your product-development process

• Responding to customer activity in your business and online to maintain an impeccable reputation

---

CHAPTER 23

IMPACT AND SATISFACTION

"Whew," said Chuck. "That sounds exhausting, but I'm glad we're here."

"Oh, we're not done yet."

"What do you mean we're not done?"

"You're about to fall into one of the classic blunders."

"I'm neither involved in a land war in Asia nor going up against a Sicilian when death is on the line," Chuck said.

"Now you're just showing off," Carole said.

"Maybe, but he's not alone. Almost every company I talk with ignores one of the most powerful resources available to them because they quit the game too soon."

"What resource is that?"

"Your customers."

"You mean the income streams?" Carole asked.

"No. The customers themselves. If you work with them this whole time, they aren't your customers. They're your friends. And friends help each other out."

"Well, friend, are you going to tell me how?" said Chuck.

"I'm sure he is," said Carole.

Here's an important secret of successful business development:

Customers like it when you listen to them, then change things based on the feedback.

Okay. So it's not *really* a secret, but it might as well be, considering how many businesses consistently fail to do this really important thing. We've talked a little about how to develop and apply customer feedback interviews to improve your products and build new ones. Now we'll look at how to apply data and do this even better.

Let's start from your own experience. Think about the last time you ordered something and it went wrong. Maybe you got onions on your burger after you asked them to hold the onions. Maybe Amazon sent you a jetpack instead of rocket skates. Whatever it was, one of three things happened:

- ✓ The vendor listened to you, was apologetic, and included you in solving the problem.

- ✓ The vendor let you speak, was apologetic, then ignored your feedback beyond the immediate moment.

- ✓ The vendor ignored your complaints.

What happened the time you're thinking about? How did that make you feel? Can you think of times the other two options happened in your life? How did those situations make you feel?

The reality is this: How you treat your existing customers and how you respond to issues and complaints can help drive your overall business development strategy. This isn't just good karma. It's a core practice of companies that want to grow with their client base, develop, and evolve. Let's look at the two most important considerations in this practice.

What Do You Ask?

When customers complain, you have a clear idea of what those customers would like to see change. When customers rave about you on

Facebook, you have a similarly clear idea of what you should keep doing. But what about moderately satisfied customers? They tend to quietly chafe under the things they would like to be different, then abandon you "by surprise" when another vendor sees and addresses their pain points.

The first step in stopping this process is to ask your clients the right questions. Over the years, we've found the following to be some of the most useful:

✓ How was your experience?

✓ What could we have done better?

✓ How did you find us?

✓ What would you google to find a business like ours?

✓ What's one thing we do better than others you do business with?

✓ What made you decide to do business with us?

✓ What is the most recent way we exceeded your expectations?

✓ What is the most recent way you became frustrated with us?

You'll notice that these questions aren't just strongly on topic. They bear three traits in common:

1. They ask about the buyer's subjective experience.
2. They are open-ended.
3. They are specific.

By crafting your questions with those three traits, you can turn a tepid and less-useful question into a source of valuable information. For example:

Bad question: What did you think of our service?

Good question: Why did you like our service?

Great question: Why did you decide to buy the upgraded package?

Asking the right questions with your customers identifies their pain points so you can solve problems early and often. It empowers your team to make the right changes at the right times. It drives innovation by identifying opportunities to make your clients even more satisfied. Asking the wrong questions wastes time in at least two ways. If you're lucky, you will only have wasted the time spent gathering the answers to the poorly structured questions. If you're *unlucky*, you will also have spent time and resources chasing bad ideas you derived from the bad questions.

How to Ask

Once you've identified the right questions to ask, your next step is to ask them at the right time and in the right way. As a customer yourself, you've already been annoyed by requests to complete an interview or fill out a survey at times when any reasonable person would realize you were too busy to do them well. Don't make that rookie mistake. Instead, apply one or both of what the research shows are the two most effective methods for gathering honest and useful information from your customers.

Triggered digital surveys are just what they sound like. An automated trigger in your CRM tells the system when a customer has reached a point in his journey where a survey is appropriate and useful. The advantages of a TDS are automation and the ability to easily onboard the results to your performance metrics, plus a strong ability to gauge customer satisfaction. The disadvantages are related to automation: You'll get fewer people actually answering your questions, and the impersonal feel is far less likely to create the personal connection necessary for turning a happy client into a dedicated brand advocate. *In general, we recommend triggered digital surveys for companies with a high number of low lifetime-value customers.*

Phone interviews are the second effective method. Keep the length to twenty to thirty minutes, since more time than that starts to build resentment in the interviewees (and often yields more information than you can effectively act on). This personal touch provides individual analysis and in-depth feedback, with opportunities to customize follow-up questions. It also establishes that connection and encourages brand advocacy. On the downside, it's time-consuming and can lead to results that are too individualized to be used company-wide. *We recommend phone interviews for companies with a small list of high lifetime-value customers.*

Customer satisfaction surveys—and your meaningful response to what they tell you—is an essential step in completing this final lap of the race.

Remember: your job isn't just to turn strangers into clients anymore. Your job isn't done until those clients[33] are vigorous evangelists for you, your team, and your product. Listening to what they tell you doesn't make that part of the job easier.

    It makes it possible.

---

33 And some folks who never even become clients.

CHAPTER 24
CUSTOMER-DRIVEN PRODUCT DEVELOPMENT

"Listen to customers," Chuck said. "That's not exactly a unique insight, Ryan."

Carole made a face. "Based on how often companies really do it, it might as well be."

"Good point," Chuck said.

"So always listen to customers," Carole said.

"Yes. And I mean always.*"*

Chuck said, "This is the place where you show us some weird but really profitable way to listen to customers that almost nobody else tries, right?"

"Well, now that you mention it ..."

Once upon a time, companies needed to spend small fortunes figuring out what new products[34] would best serve their business development. This involved deep market research, consulting with economists, hiring focus groups, and all manner of expensive, time-consuming acts that only worked about half of the time.

In the twenty-first century, your relationship with your existing customers replaces half or more of that work and expense. You have access to them like never before. Even better, they are the *perfect* testing ground for new ideas.

Why Your Client Base Is Your Best Idea Mine

You might have thought I was kidding, but seriously, you should listen to your existing customers as your first stage of R&D. Here's why:

- ✓ They know where your current products need improvement and what they wish they could buy from you (if only you offered it).

- ✓ They have a relationship with your brand, meaning they are less vulnerable to being seduced away by competitors who are developing similar products.

- ✓ If you make a product based on the feedback of an existing customer,

    - ✓ they are very likely to beta test that product and provide detailed, useful information; and

    - ✓ this increases that customer's loyalty and enthusiastic engagement. They become much more likely to transition into brand advocacy.

When you put all this together, it is like selling to an existing customer. We all know your investment is seven times more profitable when reselling than with an initial sale. Nobody's run the numbers yet,[35] but when they do, they will find that those numbers are even better

---

34 And tweaks to existing clients.
35 That I know of.

when you use existing clients, instead of random consumers, to help you develop new products.

The Right Way to Ask

Of course, all those good things I just said only work if you ask the right people in the right way at the right time. Over the years, client interviews and my own mistakes have given me a list of the most important common features of getting all of those things right.

Active Engagement Is Key

Don't wait for your clients to come to you with ideas. Actively engage in sussing out how your clients would like to see your brand grow. This seems like it would go without saying, but some people need a reminder. The purpose of this part of the customer journey is to actively listen to your customers to find out what they want next. This requires intelligent, focused attention. It is not an afterthought or rote task. Be a detective.

Read between the Lines

If you conduct in-person interviews, pay attention to voice tone, facial expressions, and body language. If you're doing email feedback, read responses for what customers might be communicating outside the actual words. In some cases, a client might have a strong opinion but be concerned about hurting your feelings. In others, they might not know exactly how to communicate their core needs. Either way, active listening techniques can help you identify the most important needs of the clients who give you feedback.

Check Your Assumptions

Every business model begins with a set of assumptions. Some examples of those assumptions might be:

✓ Our customers want this suite of options in every product.

✓ Our customers won't need or want this other suite of options.

✓ Demographic X will be the primary consumers of our product.

✓ We should focus on price point Y for what we offer.

I am consistently amazed by how many of my customers have never used their client feedback or sales metrics to fact-check their initial assumptions. Discovering and revising an incorrect core assumption can make an immense difference in your company's success and profitability.

Focus on the Story
If you can get respondents to tell you the story of their relationship with your brand, you can gather a wealth of details they wouldn't think to tell you in a shorter format. They will also answer important questions you never thought to ask. Most experts feel this is best done in in-person interviews, but even texts can tell a much richer and useful story than other forms of information-gathering.

Look Hard at Your Buying Process
There are situations in which the person making the buying decision might be different from both the person who uses your products and the person who would respond to your feedback request. Untangle this potential Gordian knot as best you can before seeking direction. An accurate answer from the wrong person points you in the wrong direction just as much as an inaccurate answer from the right person.

The Wrong Way

My experiences with this also have given me a long laundry list of how to do this wrong. A lot of it I've learned the hard way by making the mistakes myself. Some I've seen others make and have paid enough attention to learn from their misfortune. Some I've just read about in blogs or heard in podcasts, and they rang true from experiences I've had.

For worse or much worse, here are the most common mistakes I've seen in this part of profit engineering:

Limiting Responses
Limited responses (like multiple-choice surveys) are based on assumptions you make *before* listening to your clients. Instead, provide open-ended questions about a particular aspect of the experience. For example ...

✓ Describe your experience the last time you interfaced with our technical support staff.

✓ What is the most frustrating aspect of our product?

✓ Have you ever considered changing vendors? Why or why not?

✓ If we made robust changes to our product, what features would you most want us to keep?

Talking Only to Existing Customers
They are the easiest to talk with and the most likely to be on board for beta testing or buying your new offerings. But they're also the happiest people who have interacted with your company. Find ways to get feedback from the people who fell off your onboarding system. The people who *almost bought* what you offer can give you some of the most useful feedback possible about how you can improve your business.

Assuming You Understand the Customer Experience
Closely examine all of your business development and sales systems for trends indicated by the data, and then compare your findings with the actual comments of your customers. If possible, go buy what you offer from a competitor and see what it's like from the consumer side of things. Never act on what you think you know, because you understand your company from an ownership perspective.

Believing All Customers Are Created Equal
The 80/20 rule applies here. Some of your customers will provide the best feedback about how to improve what you offer. Some will be the most likely to buy your new offerings once you create them. Sometimes (rarely) these are the same people. Other customers will be perfect for helping you with new products but poor for improving existing lines. Think about how to categorize your client base so you can focus appropriately during product development efforts.

Among my beta readers, this chapter was the most surprising. Product development as (1) a kind of customer service, and (2) driven by client requests is an alien concept to many—not because it's a bad idea but simply because it's not often done.

But in this age of responsive, engaged, and opinionated consumers with a soapbox and megaphone in each pocket, it is one of the most effective ways to build a rabidly loyal following for your brand.

CHAPTER 25
REPUTATION MANAGEMENT

"But what about the bad apples?" asked Carole.

"Which bad apples?" I asked.

"The ones who spoil the barrel. We all know one loud complainer can outweigh a dozen happy customers. What do we do when things go wrong?"

"You can't please everybody," added Chuck, "and that one guy who doesn't want to be pleased can be louder than everybody else put together."

"That's true," I said.

"So what do you do about it? What do you do when you get that one howler on your social media page?"

"Well, the best plan is to do a lot of stuff before the howler shows up."

"Why?"

"You set up your social media community like we talked about earlier. That transparency and authority means people will trust you when you respond. A lot of the time, your other happy customers will do the responding for you."

"Okay. I can see that," said Chuck.

"And with that all set up, you can respond quickly and effectively to turn that bad apple into a better apple—or at least remove it from the barrel."

Once upon a time, I had a client who'd received one bad review on Google Plus. They didn't do anything about that review because it was just one person with an ax to grind.

But that one person was one of only a few reviews on G+ about their business. That bad review caused their Google performance to tank, and it cost them tens of thousands in lost revenue.

If you need me to explain why your company's reputation is important, you probably don't yet know enough about business development to benefit from this book.

But what even competent and experienced business owners don't understand is how much more important reputation is now than in previous centuries. During the bad old days, a company's greater capacity for putting information out meant a dissatisfied customer had limited ability to hurt the bottom line.

Today, an average customer or almost-customer can lambaste you via social media and negative reviews. They have the potential reach of tens of thousands, and that's assuming their comments aren't funny enough or on point enough to go viral. At the same time, more consumers use the web now to research products, brands, and companies than at any other time in history.

Bottom line: Everybody who interacts with you is talking, and everybody who *might* buy from you is listening.

Obviously, it's your job to prevent poisonous reports from entering the web by keeping everybody who comes into contact with your brand ecstatic. But modern business development requires more than not irritating your customers. You also have empowered your satisfied, ecstatic clients to share their experience via platforms like reviews, case studies, and even speaking engagements.

You need proactive reputation management.

What Is Proactive Reputation Management?

Proactive reputation management is exactly what it sounds like:

✓ Proactive—taking decisive, direct, primary action toward accomplishing a goal

✓ Reputation—impacting the words coming out of others' mouths about your company

✓ Management—directing the tone and content

Put it all together, and proactive reputation management is taking primary and direct action to manage the tone and content of what people say about your company on the web and in "real life." You do this by encouraging and making it easier for your customers to share their great experiences on third-party websites via a workflow that's triggered just like your lead and sales pipelines.

This workflow can take a variety of specific paths but generally follows the same basic steps:

✓ You request a review.

✓ The customer leaves a review.

✓ You thank the customer for the review.

Sometimes other steps are necessary. Depending on specific situations, these universal steps can look quite different from one another, but the basic structure is sound.

Reputation Management Workflows in Action

Your specific process for handling reputation management will be as unique as the lines on your palms. That said, most will fit into one of three basic workflows. Here's how each works:

Quick and Easy

Your company just finished a contract for six months of services for a local business.

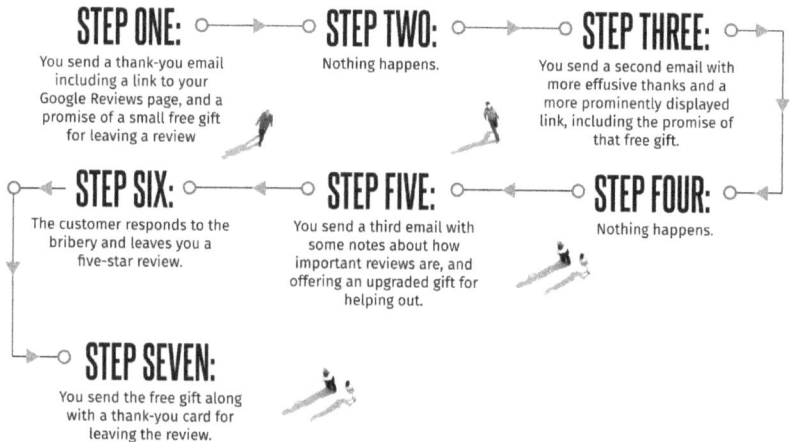

STEP ONE: ○———▶———○ **STEP TWO:** ○———▶———○ **STEP THREE:**

You send a thank-you email including a link to your Google Reviews page, and a promise of a small free gift for leaving a review.

The customer follows the link and leaves a four-star review with positive and detailed comments.

You send the free gift along with a thank-you email for leaving the review.

Everything in this workflow goes smoothly because everything goes right.

The Way of the Nag

Your company just finished a contract for six months of services for a local business.

STEP ONE: ○———▶———○ **STEP TWO:** ○———▶———○ **STEP THREE:** ○——┐

You send a thank-you email including a link to your Google Reviews page, and a promise of a small free gift for leaving a review

Nothing happens.

You send a second email with more effusive thanks and a more prominently displayed link, including the promise of that free gift.

┌——◀—— **STEP SIX:** ○———◀———○ **STEP FIVE:** ○———◀———○ **STEP FOUR:** ○——┘

The customer responds to the bribery and leaves you a five-star review.

You send a third email with some notes about how important reviews are, and offering an upgraded gift for helping out.

Nothing happens.

└——○ **STEP SEVEN:**

You send the free gift along with a thank-you card for leaving the review.

The important thing to note here is that your system already had steps three and five (and potentially seven, nine, eleven, and thirteen) in place and operating. When you make proactive reputation management part of your operations, it pays dividends. If you just leave it for the corners of your company's time, this part of your business development will never get any real traction.

Hey, What Happened?

Your company just finished a contract for six months of services for a local business.

STEP ONE:
You send a thank-you email including a link to your Google Reviews page, and a promise of a small free gift for leaving a review.

STEP TWO:
The customer follows the link, leaving a two-star rating with no commentary.

STEP THREE:
You send the free gift along with a thank-you card for leaving the review.

STEP SIX:
You enter all of the customer's concerns and complaints into your system for using the feedback to fine-tune your product, customer service, and branding.

STEP FIVE:
You move forward with the customer to continue that relationship, making all reasonable adjustments necessary to delight them.

STEP FOUR:
The point of contact for that customer makes a personal phone call, asking what happened and how your company can make it right.

Customer complaints are some of your best tools for making your brand better. Your proactive reputation management helps you tap this valuable vein of information and gives you the chance to turn that disgruntled customer into a delighted advocate by listening carefully and acting on what you've heard.

Time To Take Five

FIVE KEY TAKEAWAYS FROM THIS SECTION

☐ 1. Transparency is king, and it's okay to be human.

☐ 2. Social media and community-building need to be initiatives of their own, not afterthoughts.

☐ 3. Ask your customers questions about where to go with your brand. Interview customer frequently about what's right and what's not right. Encourage active, candid transparency.

☐ 4. Providing consistent value breeds community, as long as you tell people about it. Follow the 80/20 rule, and don't make it all about you. Be a leader in the industry.

☐ 5. Unqualified leads are a powerful source of community-building fuel.

FIVE THINGS TO DO THIS MONTH

☐ 1. Set up social media monitoring.

☐ 2. Identify your biggest pain-in-the-butt clients, and refer them to the competition.

☐ 3. Subscribe to the top-five thought leaders in your industry so you can share their blogs and thoughts.

☐ 4. Look at existing content, and set up social media sharing around it.

☐ 5. Interview your customers about what you're doing right and what you're doing wrong.

☐ 6. Interview your customers to find out their major pain points.

APPENDIX A | INSIDER'S GUIDE TO STAFFING YOUR PROFIT ENGINEERS

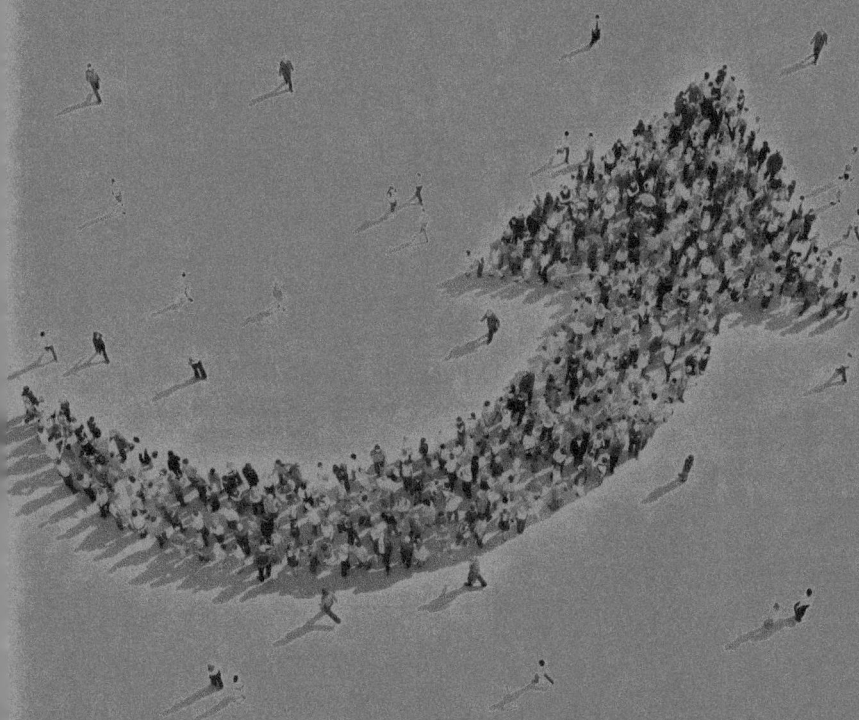

INSIDER'S GUIDE TO STAFFING YOUR PROFIT ENGINEERS

EXECUTIVE SUMMARY

In this section, we'll discuss:

- Hiring an internal profit engineering specialist vs. outsourcing to a specialist firm
- The best practices for conducting your profit engineering in-house
- How to choose a profit engineering agency

HIRING VS. OUTSOURCING YOUR PROFIT ENGINEERS

"What if I just train my team to do all of this for me? They're smart people."

"I'm sure they are. But are they passionate and engaged around this?"

"They can be."

"How sure are you about that? Good marketers are good because they're total marketing geeks."

"Watch it."

"That's not a pejorative. I'm a marketing geek. You're a software geek. Being a geek is just being unabashedly excited about the stuff that interests you."

"Okay, fair enough. I'm a geek. They're geeks."

"And so am I. The question is whether or not their geek matches the geek you need to get this particular job done. Let me ask you a few questions to help you figure out whether that's so."

This is the great debate about how to handle profit engineering for your business. Once you've decided you can't do it with the people already on your team, you have three choices:

- ✓ Hire an individual to join your company and lead your profit-engineering efforts.

- ✓ Hire an agency to provide profit engineering services for your company.

- ✓ Do neither and fail as a business.

Obviously, I don't recommend number three—but the right choice between the two remaining options is far less clear. I can't tell you which is definitively better for your business, but I can give you all the information you need to make an informed decision on your own.

Cost Analysis

Any decision based on cost requires you to run the numbers and see what the math tells you. Because I'm not necessarily writing this book in the year you'll run the numbers, we'll stay away from a detailed analysis of what things cost right now and instead walk you through the *process* for running those numbers yourself.

Step 1: Find out how much it will cost you to pay the salary of an in-house marketer with the skills you need to get an edge in your industry.

Step 2: Add the cost of your employee-benefits package.

Step 3: Add the cost of finding, processing, and training a new hire.

Step 4: Compare the total cost of steps one through three against the cost of outsourcing that same amount of work.

For example, in 2017 you could expect to spend between $80,000 and $100,000 to hire, train, and employ a senior-level marketer for one year. The cost of hiring a good marketing agency came to between $24,000 and $120,000 annually. If your employee was on the high end of that scale and your outsource option on the low end, it's a pretty compelling story. If your employee was on the low end and the agency was at the high end, the comparison is less definitive.

I'm not giving you this breakdown to replace your own research. Region and industry[36] make a huge difference in your real numbers. Instead, I want to illustrate how you might approach organizing and structuring the numbers for your own research.

Complexity and Control

If you're big into control[37], then you will probably prefer hiring an internal marketing person when it's time to up your profit engineering game. The day-to-day contact, the nature of an employee-employer relationship, and keeping everything in-house simply make control easier to achieve.

By contrast, a good agency runs the show for you. They assign out tasks to their team and yours, set agendas, think outside the box, and control the project so you don't have to. The main benefit of hiring a profit engineering firm is that it's truly a thing you shouldn't have to worry about. As a general rule, going to an outside agency means sacrificing some of your control over your marketing efforts.

Complexity is the flip side of that coin. As you might have intuited from my breakdown of expenses for an agency vs. an in-house employee, the level of complexity is much higher with the latter. You have legal factors, training, scheduling, personal concerns, *and* all the factors related to actually implementing the plans that the hire comes up with.

Using an agency makes all of the complexities their problem. Your job becomes looking at the options they recommend and then making

---

36   And, as I mentioned, what year it is.
37   And let's be honest—most successful entrepreneurs and business managers "resemble this remark."

an informed decision between those options. They handle all other aspects of your marketing.

Complexity vs. control—you can have lots of both or lots of neither. High control requires high complexity, and low control comes with reduced complexity. The balance you prefer should guide your decisions.

The Passion Question

Passion is the one place where an in-house hire unequivocally outperforms a marketing agency.

The person who is the most passionate and engaged about your business is you. The people who are the second most passionate and engaged about your business are your team members: They are the people whose paychecks depend on your business success and who see your energy and achievement on a daily basis.

A marketing agency is full of people who are passionate about *marketing* and deeply engaged in the processes and practices of what they do. They will market the heck out of your company, but they won't have your business as deeply under their skin as somebody in your house.

This doesn't mean a profit engineering agency can't do a great job, but it is a reality that should factor into your final decision.

Expertise

One of the best aspects of onboarding a new profit engineer is that they will quickly become an expert in your industry. They come to the job knowing marketing, then spend several weeks specializing in *marketing what you sell.*

Assuming the hire is successful and the fit is good, that person will become the world's leading expert in profit engineering your company, brand, and product.

When working with an agency, you have the opportunity to work with senior-level marketing professionals. Although they might not be experts in your industry *yet*, they know profit engineering cold. They can show you techniques you've never even thought of and how they have applied those techniques to help previous clients. They can provide you with the latest technology and tools and have an entire agency to give you a second and third set of eyes on everything.

As I said at the beginning of this chapter, I can't tell you which choice is right for your company.[38] But if you factor in these points and think about them in terms of your company's reality, needs, and goals, then you should be able to make the right choice on your own.

---

38   And since I run a highly successful profit engineering agency, you shouldn't trust me if I do make a recommendation.

HIRING AN
INSIDE PROFIT ENGINEER

"You've made a good case for both sides, but I'm a bit of a control freak. I like my employees on site, where I can see that they're not playing poker or watching cat videos on my dime," Chuck said.

"Fair enough. Being a control freak is a pretty common trait among successful business folks. You need at least a little of that to even want the job."

"Now comes the part where you try talking me out of it, right?"

"Nope."

"Nope?"

"Yeah, nope. Now comes the part where I share with you everything I know about how to hire the best marketer you can."

"Why would you do that?"

"Remember earlier when we talked about how a customer you don't get but who feels great about you and your company can be more valuable than a sale to somebody who's not really the right fit?"

"Yes."

"I'm okay if you're that customer. So let's talk about how, if you decide not to hire my firm, you can have success with the option that suits your needs."

So you've decided to hire a marketer, consultant, or agency—somebody to become part of your team and let everybody else see to their areas of expertise while the new hire brings in new business. This is a great move for a lot of companies but only if you do it right … because doing it wrong can be a serious problem.

Let's look at the up-front costs of hiring a new employee at the level from which you would need even a junior marketing expert to operate.

Best estimates from the MIT Sloan School of Management put training and recruiting costs alone for a new hire at just north of $9,000, plus the approximately $8,000 you'll spend on a professional salary and wages during the average ten-week time between a new hire coming on and that new hire getting up to speed. Forty-six percent of newly hired employees fail within eighteen months of being hired, and only 19 percent are fully realized successes. Putting those two numbers together shows that it will cost you nearly $20,000 to hire and train a marketer, with a 50/50 chance that they will fail before you recoup the cost.

Hiring right actually makes the cost of acquisition higher, but it can really improve those odds of success. Hiring right means asking candidates the best possible questions and knowing which questions not to ask. Though every interview, interviewer, and interviewee is different, here's a format for interviews that has worked well for us when we hire our team of marketing ninjas and inbound content whisperers:

Stage 1: Getting to Know You

I like to start with simple questions whose answers I already got in the résumé and cover letter. Things like:

- ✓ Tell me about your favorite former client.

- ✓ What did you do in your last position?

- ✓ How many years have you worked in marketing?

- ✓ When did you first start working in this industry?

- ✓ What are your favorite marketing techniques?

✓ Which marketing tools and platforms are your favorites?

✓ What's the difference between marketing and selling?

This works well for two reasons. First, it puts the candidate at ease because these are easy questions. Relaxed candidates interview better, and I hate to miss out on a great marketer just because they're also a terrible interviewee.

Second, it can weed out liars early. If the answers the candidates give in the interview don't match what they wrote on their applications, it's time to end the interview early and not waste anybody's time.

Stage 2: The What-If Game

Once we're warmed up, I move on to questions about what the candidate does or might do in different situations. This explores how they think and if their process and approach match my team, product, and audience. Some examples I like include:

✓ What resources do you use to stay up-to-date with trends and techniques?

✓ What's the coolest bit of marketing news you've heard this quarter?

✓ If I hire you, what subscription will you insist I buy?

✓ A prospect is coming in one hour from now. What benefits of our product would you use to prep them for our sales team?

✓ If I told you to redesign the company logo, what steps would you take?

✓ What about joining our team would make you happy?

Stage 3: Problem-Solving

The next set of questions looks at your candidate's past behavior, with a strong eye toward how they'll handle difficult circumstances in the future. Body language, facial expressions, and voice tone are important here since they'll give you an eye into how the interviewee responds to good and bad situations.

- ✓ What techniques do you use to work well with people who are very different from you?

- ✓ How successful are you at completing work on time with multiple projects?

- ✓ What project from the past are you most proud of?

- ✓ Tell me about a time you really screwed up and what you did to fix it.

Stage 4: Job-Related Questions

Going deeper, it's time to assess how well the interviewee actually does marketing. You'll ask a series of questions that are almost like an oral exam for a class. The goal here isn't to trick somebody with a "Ha! Gotcha!" question, but to really understand what the candidate knows about their field and what they think about key questions asked by most professional marketers.

- ✓ What metrics do you look at to assess the success or failure of a marketing campaign?

- ✓ Pick one of the metrics we talked about. Tell me what a failure by that metric might mean and what steps you would take to improve performance.

- ✓ What are the three different types of media?

- ✓ What is your general philosophy of marketing? How would you apply it to selling our product?

- ✓ There are a variety of models for the customer's journey from stranger to a client or a marketing campaign from creation to release. Choose your favorite and describe it in detail.

The Second Interview

A marketer is too important a member of your team to hire based on a single interview. Instead, set up an appointment in a week and assign the candidate homework to bring back and share. Some homework assignments that I've given in the past that helped me bring good people onto my team have included:

- ✓ A hypothetical marketing plan for our company

- ✓ A marketing brief for a specific product, type of customer, or fictitious company

- ✓ A sample of an advertisement, landing page, and messaging for a fictitious company

- ✓ An analysis of what our company could do better

For some companies, hiring an internal profit engineer is the best call. For others, hiring an external profit engineering agency is best. I can't tell you specifically which is the right call for your company.

But I can tell you that choosing to hire an internal profit engineer and then hiring the wrong person is the worst possible outcome.

CHOOSE YOUR OWN PROFIT ENGINEERING AGENCY

"I'm not saying this is one hundred percent certain, but it sounds like hiring a marketer costs me more time, money, and aggravation than bringing an outside agency on board."

"I won't argue with you there," I responded. "Plus, we're easier to fire and harder to accidentally harass."

"So we're in agreement there, but can you predict my next question?"

"Uh, is it, 'Ryan, what super-expensive restaurant should I take you to so we can celebrate hiring your company?'"

"No."

"How about, 'Ryan, why should we hire your agency out of all the agencies that claim they do what you do?'"

"Almost word for word."

"I'm not going to answer that. Instead, let me see if you can guess a question."

"Is it, 'What things should I look for when selecting an inbound marketing agency?'"

"You have been paying attention."

"It's what I do. So what's the answer?"

Every marketing agency is a brilliant collection of modern-thinking, driven, and results-oriented professionals operating at the cutting edge of technology and the absolute pinnacle of their craft.

Just ask any marketing agency.

The trouble with choosing a marketing agency is they'll all tell you they're great, and they're all trained, experienced professionals when it comes to convincing somebody that what they say is true. Few are even lying about it. It's just that a lot of the second-tier marketing agencies have drunk their own Kool-Aid so long and hard that they don't know what's really going on in marketing anymore.

Here at Nuanced Media, we've worked with hundreds of clients and heard their horror stories about the people they fired before landing happily with us. Let's look at the most important red flags that tell you an agency isn't a good match for you (or sometimes for anybody else).

Things They Say

Read[39] between the lines, analyzing how the agency talks about what they'll do for you. Beyond the old wives' advice that starts with "If it's too good to be true," watch out for these telltale talking points.

- ✓ Claiming to be generalists. Nobody can stay on top of every piece of news and new technology in every corner of modern marketing. In most cases, you're better off with a specialist who can fix up the part of your marketing that needs the most work.

- ✓ Speaking without listening. This tells you about their philosophy of marketing. Old-school marketing was exactly this, but as we've discussed, it's suicide in the social, digital, responsive age. You want an agency that listens to you, to your audience, and to the industry and market as a whole.

- ✓ Not offering proof. Can they back up claims they make about how effective their methods are? Can they physically show you successful marketing campaigns and downloadable value-added content? Without proof, there's no reason to accept their claims at face value.

---

39   And listen.

Things They Do

You're not going to catch a professional marketing agency making a big gaffe in the middle of a presentation, but watch what they do before and after the meeting. A few key points in those softer spaces can tell you more than they want you to know.

- ✓ Write poor content on their own site. Managing and producing value-added content produces some of the best standards for digital marketing. If the agency can't write great content for you, they're helping you build a frame for a house but leaving the walls to you.

- ✓ Not doing their homework. An agency should show up for your first pitch meeting having done thorough research into your industry, public marketing presence, competitors, and relevant keywords. If they come asking you for that info, they haven't done their due diligence.

- ✓ No proactivity. Whether you're currently signed or seeking a new agency, how much time goes by without a note from them? Do they actively take notes while meeting? Do they have new ideas? Proactive attitudes when they are meeting with you reflect proactive attitudes toward marketing your business … which is what you want to see.

Things They Lack

"Negative space" is a concept in art that refers to the use of empty area; examples are empty sky in a photo or white canvas in a painting. In this case, the problem with a marketing agency might not be what they are but what they aren't. Make sure the prospective agency doesn't:

- ✓ Lack experience in your industry. If you make industrial insulation, an agency that mostly helps authors promote their books won't be a good match. Neither is the other way around. Confirm that any house you work with has at least worked with clients in similar spaces.

✓ Ignore their own social media outlets. You can learn a lot about how well an agency understands social media by watching how they take care of their own brand. Lack of connection, comment response, and retweeting shows they're not following the recognized best practices.

✓ Rank low on organic search. A bit of a no-brainer, this one. If they can't make themselves rank high on organic search, how can they claim to do so for you?

✓ Lack testimonials and positive reviews. For the price a professional marketing agency charges, you should be able to expect positive word from past customers. You wouldn't buy an expensive pair of boots or new sound system without some social proof.

I'm not going to tell anybody that they absolutely need to hire a profit engineering expert. I'm not going to tell anybody that if they hire a profit engineering expert, they have to hire me.

That sort of thing is a big red flag that tells you to run away from a marketing expert of any sort.

But ...

if you choose to hire a profit engineering expert ...

and you use the advice I just gave you in this chapter ...

I'm confident you will come to the conclusion that I'm the best expert you can work with. That, or you'll find somebody at least as good for your company as I can be.

APPENDIX B | THE STUFF AT THE END

THE STUFF AT THE END

This is the stuff most people skip because it's usually about things only a few people care about. It's like the credits at the end of the movie.

But this isn't a normal-movie kind of book. This is Ferris Bueller's Day Off. It's the Marvel Expanded Universe film franchise. There's gold at the end of this rainbow—and in the middle too.

So stick around. You'll like it.

EXECUTIVE SUMMARY

In this section, we'll discuss:

- An example of what a profit engineer report looks like

- A bit more about me and how I figured out the stuff I've told you in this book

- Some ideas about how you can engage further with this book and the information it contains

IF YOU LOVED THIS BOOK...

Thank you for reading *Marketing Is Dead, Long Live Marketing: Discover the emerging marketing landscape, build effective strategies, and set your business up for success.* It was the result of over a decade of experience and research and nearly two years of writing, revising, rewriting, re-revising, re-rewriting, and general tweaking to make it as nearly perfect as possible.

If you liked it, I am very glad. If you loved it, would you be willing to do one or more of the following simple things to help ensure its success?

1. **Leave a review.** The more reviews that are left for a book on Amazon.com, the more juice Amazon's search algorithms give that title. Leaving a positive review helps get this book in more hands. A similar (even identical) review on Goodreads.com helps guide readers directly to the title.

2. **Lend it to a friend.** I don't need to sell this book to make my goals happen. That's not what it's about. But I do need people to read it and engage around the ideas. Lend your copy to a friend or buy it as a gift to help get the word out.

3. **Connect with me.** You can find me on Facebook, LinkedIn, and Twitter. I'll answer your questions and consider your advice, and I promise not to cry if you have some constructive criticism.

Thank you again. My ideas only matter to the extent that people engage around them.

PREFACE
WHY I WROTE THIS BOOK

After losing $300,000 founding and ultimately destroying my first company by doing everything wrong, I have dedicated my life to doing business better, smarter, and faster. During my time at Nuanced Media, we have applied a few lean strategies that focus on the 20 percent that creates 80 percent of the ROI. This includes challenging the existing thought process regarding marketing and business development, implementing the scientific method so we are constantly improving in a trackable manner, and focusing on what really matters—the profitability of our partners' businesses. In the new digital business-development world, systems and infrastructure are being established that can be tested and optimized, which ultimately lead to a sustainable strategic advantage for industry leaders. As we have recently seen with the manufacturing industry's automation to reduce cost and increase efficiency and revenue, the same is occurring with businesses throughout the world.

This book is intended to be an introduction to some of the new methods and philosophies of digital business development/profit engineering. We are in the middle of a very large paradigm shift, and one needs to start at the beginning.

www.ingramcontent.com/pod-product-compliance
Lightning Source LLC
Chambersburg PA
CBHW040754220326
41597CB00029BA/4807

FINAL THOUGHTS

The ACME Company Report

A picture is worth a thousand words, but an example is worth a thousand pictures.

You've noticed throughout this book that we've used an imaginary conversation between yours truly and the ACME Company.

If you search this link https://grow.nuancedmedia.com/acme-report/, you can download a copy of a real report done for that imaginary company. It's the same as what we do during our initial intake and analysis for any real client. Reading it can help you digest and better understand the ideas at work in what you just read.

It can also help you walk yourself through an initial intake and analysis report to better position your company to use the profit engineering method, with or without our help.

ABOUT THE AUTHOR

Ryan Flannagan has more than fifteen years of business development, marketing, and operational experience. He has worked with hundreds of companies to establish best practices, focusing on the 20 percent that produces 80 percent of the revenue. He has been a lifelong entrepreneur. It all started with a pooper-scooper business at age eight, in which he employed neighborhood children to complete the scooping of poop, which his mother quickly made him shut down.

During his tenure at Nuanced Media, he has built a client base that represents a total revenue of over $1.5 billion. To date, Nuanced Media's biggest accomplishment has been making a client $18.5 million in a five-week period, for 5,200 percent ROI.

He is happily married to his wife, Bianka, and is the proud father of their daughter, Brynn. He enjoys hiking, meditation, perpetual learning, and being a strong community steward and a good friend. He received his master's degree in business from Washburn University and his bachelor's degree in the arts for communication and Spanish from the University of Arizona.

Time To Take Five

FIVE KEY TAKEAWAYS FROM THIS SECTION

- [ ] 1. Closing is an art. It should be custom-designed to match each organization.
- [ ] 2. You're only as good as the systems you put in place.
- [ ] 3. Knowledge management is the brain and execution of your company.
- [ ] 4. You're only as good as your numbers. Your numbers are only as good as how closely you examine them.
- [ ] 5. B2B closing in this century is too complex to do well without systems in place.

FIVE THINGS TO DO THIS MONTH

- [ ] 1. Identify the next-step goal for every stage of your sales funnel.
- [ ] 2. Run through each stage of your pipeline to make sure that it's easy and intuitive to get from start to finish for somebody unfamiliar with the system.
- [ ] 3. Identify the three things that differentiate your best customers from the others.
- [ ] 4. Have a friend cold-call your team and report on the experience.
- [ ] 5. Find your "Bobs"—your points where the fastest source of information is to "ask Bob." Target those for immediate systematization.

SECTION 4 | DELIGHTING

DELIGHTING

BUSINESS SCHOOL DEFINITION

Turning customers into brand advocates -people who talk favorably about a brand or product, then pass on positive word-of-mouth messages to other people

PROFIT ENGINEERING DEFINITION

The strategy of using blogs, webinars, and excellent service to take unqualified leads past the stage of being clients and into the zone of vigorous brand advocacy

> *Customer and employee referrals have the highest close rate compared to any other business development channel. Additionally, new prospects trust online reviews as much as a personal referral 66% of the time. Perfecting this phase of your funnel can grow your business by orders of magnitude.*